I Like My Dog Until I Don't

A Comprehensive but Simple Guide to Real-Life Dog Training

Copyright Page

This book is a work of original nonfiction, drawing on the author's personal experiences and professional practice. While the content was independently written and does not rely on direct quotations or citations, the author acknowledges the valuable influence of various books and thought leaders in the field of dog training. A full list of these works can be found in the *Reference* section.

For information, permission requests, or speaking inquiries, please contact:
Aaron A. Lee
Email: info@pawfectpracticetraining.com

Cover design by: **Aaron A. Lee**

Published by Honey & Ivery Publishing

Pawfect Practice Publishing, an imprint of Honey & Ivory Publishing

Sacramento, California

ISBN (Paperback): 979-8-9935122-0-4
ISBN (Hardcover): 979-8-9935122-2-8
ISBN (Signed Limited Hardcover): 979-8-9935122-3-5
ISBN (eBook): 979-8-9935122-1-1

Library of Congress Control Number: 2025910965

Printed in the United States of America
First Edition, 2025

Disclaimer

This book is intended for educational and informational purposes only and is based on the author's experience as a dog trainer. The techniques, tools, and recommendations described are provided as general guidance and may not be suitable for every dog or situation.

Results may vary significantly depending on the individual dog, its environment, training history, and the consistency and skill of the handler. The author and publisher make no guarantees regarding behavioral outcomes or the effectiveness of the training methods discussed.

By using the information in this book, you agree to assume full responsibility for the safety and behavior of your dog. Always use caution, common sense, and prioritize safety when working with animals. The author disclaims any liability for injury, loss, or damage caused directly or indirectly by the use or misuse of this material.

This book is not intended to replace professional veterinary advice, medical guidance, or in-person training when necessary. When in doubt, consult a qualified professional.

Special thank you to Paula for spending countless nights helping me edit and proofread this line by line.

Numerous clients and their dogs inspired this book over the years. Thank you for entrusting me with the chance to help you on your training journey. It was my honor to learn and help every one of you.

This book is dedicated to my lovely dogs, who made me the trainer I am today. Without the experiences and lessons you gals taught me, I wouldn't be anything.

-Aaron A. Lee

♨ Tools to Make This Work in Real Life

This book provides structure, tools, and a no-BS approach to dog training. But let's be real: Flipping back and forth through pages while holding a tug toy in one hand and a treat in the other isn't always practical.

So, I put together a free resource page just for readers of this book. You will find:

- Printable versions of all the worksheets (yes, the same ones in the book).

- Full-color visuals of hand signals and training aids

- Video demos for key commands — so you can *see* what the drills look like.

- Bonus material that grows over time based on real feedback from real owners.

🔗 **https://bit.ly/ilikemydogbookresources**

▣ **Scan the QR code below to get started**

No email walls. No sales pitch. Just useful stuff to help you get better results and make training actually stick.

Because owning a dog isn't about perfection, it's about showing up, doing the work, and building something real.

Table of Contents

Introduction

All great books begin with a story from the author's life, and this one is no different. Although this is a dog training book, it's also a story of growth, challenges, and self-discovery. Growing up, we had no pets, except for fish (which, let's be honest, don't really count). My mother had a deep fear of dogs, so my exposure to them was limited. However, when my sister moved out, she had a dog, a Shih Tzu mix named Gentleman. I quickly became enamored with him, spending every possible moment with him, even doing extra sleepovers at her apartment. That was my first real experience with dogs, and the foundation for my future in dog training, even if I didn't know it at the time.

I didn't realize it then, but I was unknowingly learning about capturing behaviors, shaping behaviors with rewards, and timing those rewards, all fundamental aspects of dog training. Yet, it wasn't until years later that I would be able to put these lessons into practice.

Fast forward to my early twenties, I found myself in my first apartment far away from home. I had no idea what I was doing with my life, but I thought it would be a good idea to get a dog. That's right! I was working part-time with no real experience with dog ownership and no clear plan. But I REALLY wanted a dog. Luckily, I figured it out along the way. While working as a vendor for a pet food company at a rescue event in Yuba City, California, I adopted Onyx, a terrier mix. I had about $83 to my name at the time, and the adoption fee was $50, plus a small bag of food and treats. Despite the limited funds, I became the proud owner of my first dog, Onyx—15 pounds of courage and attitude, with a walk to match.

Onyx wasn't just a dog; she was one of two that would teach me what I needed to know to become a dog trainer. But this book isn't just about the good things; I'll share the struggles, too. Getting Onyx reignited my passion for dogs, and the lessons I learned with her set me on a path that would lead me to becoming a professional dog trainer.

About a year after I adopted Onyx, I decided to get another dog—my first puppy, Omni. Omni was a shepherd mix, energetic, sweet, and full of love. She would play an important role in shaping my approach to training and my understanding of the challenges dog owners face. I've dedicated a chapter to "Onyx and Omni," where I'll share the lessons I learned from them.

Now, enough with memory lane—let me share the story that truly opened my eyes to the responsibilities of dog training. Picture this: I'm at a beautiful campground in California's rolling hills and mountains. It's early autumn, and around 1 PM, I've just arrived, unpacked, and set up my campsite. I let Onyx and Omni out to relieve themselves (Onyx was about 2 years old, and Omni about 1). At the time, I was in my mid-twenties, feeling like a hotshot novice dog trainer—full of confidence but lacking real experience. I had done some training with a mentor and was now venturing out on my own.

I had both dogs on a picnic table doing a rug-wait (which is a place command) while I finished setting up my tent. Omni, a 60-pound shepherd mix, was sweet and energetic, but also strong and built like a tank. As I worked, I noticed someone walking their small dog across the campsite, about 30 yards away. In the blink of an eye, Omni took off toward the owner and his dog at full speed. The owner froze, and I panicked. I called out to Omni, hoping she would listen. The seconds felt like an eternity. But just about 10 yards from the owner, Omni did a large U-turn and came back to me. My heart was racing, and I was relieved—but I also learned something invaluable. This experience humbled me. It taught me that dog training isn't just about commands; it's about taking responsibility for your dog's actions, understanding leash management, and always putting safety first. My poor judgment that day didn't just put the owner and their dog at risk; it also put Omni in danger.

It's been 10 years since that day, and I've learned a great deal since then. I've opened and operated a successful dog training business and worked for two established companies in the field of dog training. I always share that story with clients to stress the importance of training, but more importantly, to emphasize which commands are the most important.

As you read through this book, my goal is to pass along the knowledge, experience, and philosophies I've gained over the years. This book is designed to be a comprehensive guide to dog training, helping to strengthen the bond between you and your dog. It's broken into three parts: canine learning theory, behavior modification, and the practical application and proofing of commands. My goal is to offer an easy-to-understand methodology that can be applied to any command or behavior you want to train.

Keep in mind, every dog is different and unique, and that's the joy of training. Think of dog training like a professional contractor building a house—various tools are needed for different jobs. The techniques and approaches you use must be tailored to the individual dog in front of you. I also recommend seeking professional guidance when necessary. This book isn't meant to replace a local trainer's expertise; it's simply a supplemental guide to enhance your understanding of dog training and ownership.

Before we dive into the main content, I want to stress something crucial: there are no "bad dogs." Let me say that again: bad dogs don't exist. What we have are dogs with behaviors that haven't been shaped to fit into the human world. How would they know what's acceptable in our society? How are they supposed to understand that a $200 pair of shoes isn't a chew toy, or that the food on the table is off-limits? Yes, some dogs do things that are unpleasant or dangerous, but they never do so out of malice. Dogs, like all animals, operate on a basic level of survival— looking for food, water, safety, or comfort. When you take on the responsibility of dog ownership, remember that it's your job to help them navigate our world, teaching them the behaviors they need to live safely and happily in it.

Using this Guide

Let me start by saying thank you for taking the time to use my book on your dog training journey. I'd like to offer some tips on how to make the most of this book. I tried to write something easy to follow and that engages the reader. My goal was to strike a balance between the technical aspects of dog training and my personal experience. I understand that for some of you, this might be your first dog, or maybe you are struggling with some bad habits. This might be the book that inspires you to compete or take your dog training to the next level. This book is broken into three different parts. Each offers something valuable. The first part covers the foundation of dog ownership, including topics like routines, personal stories, and lessons learned from my dogs. The second part is designed to cover training techniques, methods, and give detailed instructions on training my *'primary commands all dogs should know.'* The third part goes into details about proofing behaviors to make sure they stick. Let me be honest. Dog training is a complete science. You can pick any topic and write an entire book on just that. I didn't want to write something that would be so dense that it wasn't helpful, so I did the best I could to condense all aspects of dog training. The book ends with worksheets to help guide you through training commands and some of my favorite games and drills for training. So given that format, the parts of this book can be looked at as standalone, even though they build upon one another. You cannot 'proof' a behavior without first training the behavior, and having a routine makes training a lot easier. However, maybe you just need help with routines, or maybe you want to learn about training. I hope that you read the book from cover to cover, but I also want you to know this isn't a novel, so feel free to jump around, make notes, and move along at your own pace. I have included a free online resource that provides worksheets and demonstration videos to be used alongside this book.

▶ Get the printable version and demo video:
https://bit.ly/ilikemydogbookresources

Before We Begin: Understanding Training Concepts

There are many terms in this book that might be new to some of you. So, I wanted to define some of them before we get started as a reference guide to make following the content easier. I have also included at the end of the book a comprehensive glossary of dog training terms. Some of the terms in the glossary might not be used in the book, but I wanted to provide as much information as I can, especially if you find yourself viewing one of my videos that uses one of those terms. I also encourage you all to check out the references at the end of the book. I included some of my favorite books about dog training, which I have learned from in some capacity on my journey.

- **Positive Reinforcement** – Rewarding a behavior to increase the likelihood it will occur again.
- **Shaping** – Gradually reinforcing behaviors that approximate the desired behavior.
- **Luring** – Using a treat or object to guide a dog into a desired position or behavior.
- **Capturing** – Reinforcing a behavior the dog naturally offers on its own.
- **Marking** – Using a word (e.g., "Yes!") or clicker to mark the moment a dog does the correct behavior.
- **Disengagement** – Teaching the dog to break focus and move away from something voluntarily.
- **Recall** – The act of a dog returning to the handler when called.
- **Proofing** – Testing behaviors among six different criteria (e.g., duration, distance, distraction, latency, precision, and speed) to strengthen behavior reliability.
- **Threshold** – The dog's limit for tolerance or stress before reacting.
- **Over-arousal** – A heightened emotional state that interferes with learning or response.
- **Trigger Stacking** – When multiple stressors build up, it often leads to a reactive response.
- **Reactivity** – Over-responsive behavior to a stimulus (e.g., barking/lunging at dogs or people).
- **Impulse Control** – The ability of a dog to resist temptation or delay gratification.

Training Tools & Methods

- **6 ft Leash** - A standard dog leash that is six feet long, commonly made of nylon or leather.
- **Long Line** – A long training leash, typically longer than 15 ft, used for training (i.e., building recall at a distance).
- **High-Value Reward** – A treat or toy that is especially motivating to the dog.

- **Clicker** – A tool used for marking behavior with a sound.
- **Leash Pressure** – gentle tension on the leash used for communication to guide a dog's movement or prompt a response, such as moving toward the handler, slowing down, or yielding attention.

Learning Mechanics

- **Cue** – A signal given to prompt a specific behavior.
- **Latency** – The time between giving a cue and the dog performing the behavior.
- **Generalization** – The dog's ability to perform a behavior in different environments or situations.
- **Desensitization** – Gradual exposure to a stimulus to reduce a negative response.
- **Counterconditioning** – Changing a dog's emotional response to a stimulus by associating it with something positive.

Behavioral Terms

- **Engagement** – When a dog voluntarily pays attention to the handler.
- **Displacement Behavior** – Actions like sniffing or scratching that can indicate stress or conflict.
- **Flight Distance** – The space a dog needs to feel safe.
- **Body Language** – Posture, tail, ears, and facial expressions that communicate the dog's emotional state.

Part 1:

Trust is the foundation built on consistency

How it Starts

Ideally, before bringing a dog home, you've done your research. You know the breed's temperament, health concerns, exercise needs, and life expectancy. That's the best-case scenario—but let's be honest, it rarely happens that way.

More often, someone sees a dog they admire, maybe a friend's well-behaved dog, a movie star pup, or the breed they always wanted as a kid, and that sparks the desire to get one. So, they start searching for the perfect match. Sometimes they get lucky and find it. But in many cases, they end up at a shelter and settle on something close enough. It may look like the breed, but it comes with surprises.

Let's look at two common scenarios.

In the first scenario, someone does everything right on paper. They research German Shepherds in-depth, learning about their temperament, health concerns, exercise needs, and ideal living conditions. They buy the supplies, read the books, and feel fully prepared. But instead of finding a puppy, they adopt an older dog that resembles a German Shepherd. From day one, things feel off. The dog has a past, comes with unwanted habits, and doesn't match the expectations of the owner.

In the second scenario, someone does not research at all. They want a German Shepherd but decide to wing it. They end up with a puppy that looks similar, only to discover it's a Belgian Malinois. For those who don't know, Malinois are incredibly intelligent, driven, and often too much for a first-time dog owner. Within weeks, the cute puppy becomes a handful.

Now, both owners have good intentions. But who's better equipped for the challenge ahead? The one with breed knowledge and an older dog, or the one with a puppy of a completely different breed?

The answer? **It doesn't come down to the owner, it comes down to the dog.** Every dog is different. Breed matters, yes, but so does age, background, and individual temperament. It's the classic nature vs. nurture conversation. Even two puppies from the same litter can grow up with completely different personalities, learning styles, and behavior challenges.

The typical journey to dog ownership often begins with acquiring a dog from a family member or friend. Maybe someone found a stray, or you simply went to the shelter and rescued a pup without considering the breed. In the beginning, everything seemed perfect. The first four weeks are like the honeymoon phase of any relationship. Your dog is perfect, and everything is smooth sailing. This phase is common for almost every new dog and their family. However, after about three months, the challenges begin.

The first time your dog sees a squirrel, interacts with other dogs, or must be left alone, things start to shift. Here's the truth: training began long before your dog came home. Every interaction you have with your dog from the moment you meet, teaches them something about you, just as much as it teaches you about them.

As we move through this book, I want to emphasize that one of the most critical parts of training is the foundation you set from the very beginning. This foundation is built on trust, and trust is established through consistent, reliable behavior. The way you communicate with your dog—through tone, frequency, and body language—sends messages, sometimes without you even realizing it.

It might sound funny, but in a way, you are setting an example of how consistent your dog must be in their behavior. How well do you stick to your training, walking, and feeding schedules?

When your puppy first jumps on you, it may be cute, right? Do you tolerate the behavior and even praise it? Or when your puppy grabs a sock or shoe, and runs around with it, it's funny because the item might be insignificant at the time. Besides, how cute is a puppy dragging a shoe around that's way too big for them? We often think it's a harmless joke, one that they'll grow out of as they mature. And sure, they might, but for your dog, this could be the beginning of resource guarding or other unwanted behaviors. What's cute in a 5-pound puppy can quickly become a problem when that same pup grows into a 65-pound adolescent.

So, is it fair to change the rules later? Think about it like this: If your boss asked you to come to work at 7 am every day for a month, then suddenly your schedule changes to 6:30 am without notice. Also, you get written up for being late. How would that make you feel?

Now, I want to make it clear: communicating with a dog and building trust is much more complex than simply sending an email. But the point remains that being consistent and clear with your dog is key to building that trust. This is why it's so important to know exactly what information you're conveying and to ensure you're sending the right message.

Throughout this book, I'll share rules that I've learned from mentors and developed over my years of experience as a dog trainer. Rule #1: Never lie to your dog. This might sound strange, so let me explain. What does it mean to lie to a dog? It's simple: don't change the rules. If you allow your dog on the furniture and then, after buying a new expensive couch, you suddenly scold your dog for jumping on it, you've lied to them. You've broken the consistency that your dog relies on.

Take a moment to think about the 5 house rules you have for your dog. These rules should be agreed upon by everyone in your household. Discuss them as a group, and make sure everyone is on the same page. I've provided a sample list of house rules below (feel free to adopt these or come up with your own). These rules should be established *before* your dog comes home, and once you've set them, you must stick to them. Consistency is key.

Creating Your Dog's House Rules

Use the worksheet below to establish your dog's house rules. There you'll see an example for guidance, and in the blank spaces you can write your own rules and enforcement strategies.

House Rule #1:
Example: *No jumping on people*

Part 1

How to enforce: *Reinforcing polite greeting manners by rewarding 'sit' when greeting.*

Your Rule: _____

How to Enforce This Rule: _____

House Rule #2:
Example: *Stay off the furniture*
How to enforce: *Reinforcing my dog when all four paws are on the floor, or when they are lying in their appropriate location (bed/cot).*

Your Rule: _____

How to Enforce This Rule: _____

House Rule #3:
Example: *No stealing food or items*
How to enforce: *Reinforcing my dog for appropriate kitchen etiquette and not allowing access to counters.*

Your Rule: _____

How to Enforce This Rule: _____

House Rule #4:
Example: *Sit and wait for meals.*
How to enforce: *My dog must sit and wait for me to release them before they eat their meals.*

Your Rule: _____

How to Enforce This Rule: _____

House Rule #5:
Example: *No digging in the yard*
How to enforce: *Provide mental and physical stimulation, limit alone time in the backyard, and create an area that is dog-friendly and safe.*

Your Rule: _____

How to Enforce This Rule: _____

Part 1

Additional Notes (Optional):

_____

_____

Tips for Success:

- Ensure everyone in your household is on board with the house rules.
- Stick to your rules consistently to communicate expectations.
- Be patient and allow your dog time to adjust to the rules.

Once you've set the house rules, **stick to them — not just for a few weeks or months, but for the life of your dog**. Of course, life happens, and some things may change. But as the leader of your pack, your job is to anticipate and prepare for those changes before they happen. That's why it's important not to create rules that are likely to change later.

Let me give you a fictional example. Meet Rick, a new dog owner who just brought home his pup, Fido. Rick is single, and he enjoys having Fido sleep in the bed with him. It's cozy, it's bonding — no problem. Fast forward a few years, and Rick starts dating someone. Now there are two humans and one dog sharing the bed, and suddenly, space becomes an issue. Fido is no longer allowed on the bed. The rules have changed.

To us, this might seem like a small and necessary adjustment. But for Fido, it's confusing and disappointing. He doesn't understand why the rules changed or what he did wrong. If this kind of inconsistency happens repeatedly, your dog may begin to question whether they can rely on you to meet their needs. **This is how trust breaks down — not in big dramatic moments, but in the little things that pile up over time.**

On the flip side, a dog that can trust its owner will go the extra mile. A trusting dog is more eager to listen, more confident, and less prone to behavior issues.

Once the rules are agreed upon, the next step is to set up a consistent **training and stimulation schedule**. Dogs need daily mental and physical exercise to stay balanced. This isn't just about burning energy — it's about keeping their brains engaged and their behavior stable. You may hear a lot of myths about dogs, but here's one thing that's always true:

-A bored dog is a destructive dog.

Feeding

Before I provide the daily schedule, I want to break down each component in detail to give you some helpful context. First up, **feeding**. It's one of the most overlooked opportunities for training and enrichment, but it plays a crucial role in building structure, trust, and good habits with your dog.

Let's start with something simple: having a **consistent feeding schedule** is crucial. Dogs thrive in predictable environments. Feeding time isn't just about calories, it's a moment for structure, discipline, and a chance to teach polite behaviors. You'll hear this theme a lot throughout this book: **structure builds trust, and trust builds better behavior**.

Most people feed their dogs twice a day (some feed three times). Regardless of frequency, each meal is a chance to reinforce good manners. But first, let's address a common mistake: **free feeding** and why I strongly recommend avoiding it.

The Problem with Free Feeding

Free feeding is exactly what it sounds like, leaving food out all day so your dog can graze whenever they like. Some people fill the bowl once daily, others top it off when it looks low. It might seem convenient to have one less thing to remember on a busy schedule, but here's the issue:

Free access to food devalues that resource.

Let me put this in human terms. Imagine Rick (our favorite fictional dog owner) has a job that pays a decent salary. But Rick also has a bucket of cash at home that magically refills itself daily, no matter what he does. How long do you think Rick will keep showing up to work? Probably not long. After all, why work for something you can get for free?

Now think about your dog. If you're leaving food out all day, you're removing one of the most powerful motivators you have for training: **earning resources**. If food just *appears*, why should your dog sit, stay, or come when called for a treat later?

Free feeding also makes **potty training** harder. If you don't know when food goes in, it's tough to predict when it comes out. Structure helps manage accidents and build consistent potty routines.

Feeding as a Foundation

I'm not here to prescribe a specific diet that's a conversation for your veterinarian. The information here is for healthy dogs without medical restrictions. Once you've settled on the right food and feeding frequency, **mealtime becomes a daily training opportunity**.

Here are just a few things you can reinforce around feeding:

- Waiting patiently before eating (impulse control)
- Sitting for meals (polite behavior)
- Releasing on command (structure and clarity)
- Associating meals with calm behavior (mental conditioning)

Feeding time becomes more than just routine; it becomes a **foundation for communication, expectation, and mutual respect**.

Impulse Control at Mealtime

So, you're on board with no free feeding. You have a schedule. But what if your dog is diving into the bowl before it even hits the ground? Or jumping impatiently while you prepare the food?

This is where **impulse control** comes in.

I believe that 90% of bad behavior could be improved through impulse control management. Dogs live in the *now*. They don't care about tomorrow or your weekend plans. For them, food is a limited, survival-based resource, not something that arrives automatically every month from your Chewy subscription.

Part 1

So, this is a great moment to **teach patience**.

Start with a simple "sit" command. Your dog should maintain the sit while you:

1. Prepare the food
2. Place the bowl on the floor or stand
3. Step away from the bowl
4. Give a clear release command to start eating

Let me be clear: **this isn't about dominance**. This is about teaching calm behavior and setting expectations. Having your dog wait 30–60 seconds before eating can build habits that carry into commands like *stay* and *wait*.

Believe it or not, at this point, you've already started training just by feeding with purpose.

Everything Is Training

This is a great time to revisit a key idea: **everything you do with your dog is training**. Every interaction is data your dog uses to understand the world. They're always learning what behavior gets what result.

Here's an example: the classic **mailman effect**.

Dogs bark. But they *really* bark at delivery people. Why? Because every day, the mail carrier comes, your dog barks, and then the person leaves. To the dog, that barking worked! This unintentionally reinforces reactive behavior.

Now imagine this happening daily while you're at work. You never see it. But this behavior is becoming a habit, and your dog is learning without your input.

Even something as simple as feeding can have layers of impact on your dog's behavior. But don't worry, we'll get through it together.

Part 1

Setting a Feeding Schedule

So, we've agreed: free feeding is out, scheduled feeding is in.

But how rigid should that schedule be?

Let's say you normally feed your dog at 7:00 a.m., but today you're running late and feed at 9:00 a.m. What's the harm, right? Consistency **matters**. Dogs, like us, thrive on routine. A regular schedule helps with:

- Predictable potty routines
- Noticing early signs of illness (loss of appetite, etc.)
- Starting the day with a win (structure = success)

And how long should a dog have access to their food?

My general rule: about **5 minutes longer than their typical eating time**. If your dog usually takes 15 minutes, give them 20. After that, the bowl comes up. This keeps food valuable and prevents grazing habits.

Also important: your dog should be **comfortable with food being taken away**. This does **not** mean grabbing the bowl mid-meal — that's unsafe and unnecessary. But they should be able to finish calmly, sit, and allow you to remove the bowl.

Advanced dogs can even be called away from the bowl or tolerate a hand near their food. But these exercises should always be supervised and done with professional guidance, especially if food aggression is present.

Recap: What Have We Learned?

- Feeding is an opportunity to build **trust** and **structure**
- Free feeding removes a key resource for training
- Scheduled feeding improves behavior, potty training, and predictability
- Waiting before eating teaches **impulse control**
- Every interaction with your dog is a **training moment**
- Feeding time should start and end with **polite, calm behavior**

Part 1

Hand Feeding

Yes, we're still talking about food, and this next concept might be unpopular: **hand feeding**.

Yes, it's messy. Yes, it's time-consuming. But for **new dogs and puppies**, this is one of the **best bonding tools** I've used.

Obvious disclaimer: don't try this with a dog that has a history of biting or food aggression. Always prioritize safety.

But for puppies and young adult dogs, hand feeding helps:

- Build trust
- Reinforce patience
- Teach that human hands = rewards

I use this method during the first month with any new dog. I hand-feed **half of each meal**, and the rest goes in the bowl. It's a soft, early introduction to all the habits and rules around food, and it sets the tone for our relationship.

Feeding Without a Bowl

Finally, let's get more creative: **ditch the bowl entirely**.

There's a saying: *"Placing food in front of a dog that the dog didn't work for is considered a rude gesture."* Whether that's true or not, the idea behind it is solid: dogs love a challenge.

There are tons of **food-dispensing toys** like:

- **Buster Cube**
- **Kong Wobbler**

These toys make dogs work a little for their food by rolling, nudging, or pawing them around. It's a combination of mental and physical stimulation, which is **fantastic enrichment**.

Part 1

You still want to maintain structure during setup:

- Prep the toy
- Ask for polite behavior
- Set it down, then release dog to eat

And don't worry if they don't know how to use it at first, dogs need to be **shown how to play**. Spend a couple of weeks modeling the toy's function and supporting them until they get it.

Kibble as Rewards

Another option? Use your dog's kibble as **training rewards** throughout the day.

If you're training twice a day (as recommended), this easily becomes **scheduled feeding + structured training**. It also overlaps with hand feeding and gives the dog multiple enrichment points during the day.

Remember: **consistency is key**. Your dog's behavior is a direct reflection of what they've learned from you and what they've been allowed to get away with.

Final Thoughts

When we provide food, water, shelter, and protection, we start to create a **hierarchy within the bond** that's not based on dominance but based on trust.

I don't subscribe to dominance theory. Your dog isn't trying to "be the alpha." They just want to know what to expect and how to behave, and if sitting calmly gets them food, that's a deal they're happy to make. Even if it takes a bit for them to understand.

So, feed with intention, train with purpose, and enjoy the process.

Part 1

Enrichment

Now let's move along to one of my favorite pieces of the schedule: **enrichment**! This is where we add fun, creativity, and challenges into a dog's daily routine. Activities that stimulate them physically, mentally, and emotionally. Sometimes, a single activity hits all three at once, which is a win in my book.

Enrichment is a great opportunity to be creative. Sure, you can invest in puzzles, games, and toys specifically designed for dogs, and there are tons out there. However, you can also DIY puzzles with simple household items to create fun, constructive outlets for your pup. I love enrichment because it builds independence and self-confidence in dogs. Giving your dog problems to solve works their brain, and surprisingly, mental stimulation is often more exhausting than physical activity.

You've probably heard the saying: **"A bored dog is a destructive dog."** And it's true. A dog without enough mental and physical outlets will start making up games… like rearranging the stuffing in your couch cushions, or taste-testing every pair of shoes in your closet. While proper puppy-proofing and setting up a safe, designated area can help, most of us give our dogs too much freedom too soon, and that's when the trouble begins.

So, plan ahead. Before you even bring your dog home, think about when you'll provide enrichment throughout the day. I recommend having at least **3 to 4 different types of puzzles or activities** on hand so that you can rotate to keep things fresh and engaging. These are great for dogs of all ages. The more you plan your dog's day, the less chance they have to get bored and destructive.

Remember earlier when I mentioned ditching the food bowl? Using a **Buster Cube** or **treat-dispensing toy** to feed your dog is enrichment. You're combining mealtimes with mental stimulation — and that's exactly what enrichment is all about.

At its core, enrichment allows dogs to tap into their natural instincts. This is why it's important to understand your dog's breed traits and tendencies. If your dog is bred for scent work, try hiding treats around the house for them to find. If your dog is a heavy chewer or tends to be mouthy, offer toys or games that satisfy that need safely and appropriately.

A lot of so-called "bad behaviors" are just normal dog behaviors — they're only inconvenient for us humans. Dogs interact with the world by chewing, sniffing, barking, chasing, jumping — but most of the time, we don't give them proper outlets for any of those. Enrichment is how we bridge that gap. And yes, sometimes we must get a little creative.

For example, it's not fair to expect a dog not to chew. Chewing helps them keep their teeth healthy and soothes their gums, especially during teething. If my dog goes after a table leg, I don't get mad. I take that as communication: **"Hey, I need something to gnaw on."** So, I redirect them to a durable chew instead. If they're grabbing socks or blankets, I offer a soft toy. These behaviors also give me feedback. If my dog is seeking out inappropriate items, it might be a sign they need more enrichment, more training, or more exercise.

Enrichment Ideas

I recommend aiming for **30 to 45 minutes of enrichment twice a day**. And these don't have to be complicated.

Let's say you're sitting down to eat, taking a call, or focusing on work. Your dog starts whining — but you know they're not hungry, they've gone potty, and they're not hurt. That's a great moment to hand them a **knucklebone, Kong**, or **chew toy** to keep them entertained while you handle your task.

Another scenario: you've got guests coming over and want to prevent your dog from jumping and barking at them. Try putting your dog in their safe area with a **Buster Cube** or puzzle feeder. While they're working for their food, your guests can arrive peacefully — no chaos at the door.

Some enrichment activities involve us, but many don't. **Fetch** is a classic example that builds a bond between a human and a dog. Sure, there are automated ball launchers, but honestly, they can take away from the spirit of the game. Sometimes, human interaction is the whole point.

Here is one more game that can save your furniture and your sanity. If you are heading out for a bit, try setting up a designated dog area that is safe. Now, try placing **"hiding treats"** around that area before you leave. You can even leave a "treat treasure," something high-value like a bully stick, for your dog to discover while you are gone. This not only keeps them busy but can also help reduce separation anxiety when used consistently and thoughtfully.

Walking

By now, we understand the importance of feeding as more than just a meal, it's a time to reinforce calm, polite behavior and even squeeze in a mini-training session. We've also covered how enrichment supports a dog's mental, physical, and emotional needs while building confidence and channeling energy in a productive way. Now let's talk about another foundational part of your dog's daily routine: **the walk**.

Much like feeding, we all agree on how essential walking is for a dog's health and happiness. But what often gets overlooked is the *type* of walk we give and the *standards* we set for each outing. While I'll go into more detail in part two — including types of walks, how long they should be, and specific leash drills — here we'll focus on walking as it relates to daily structure and scheduling.

Every dog should have a daily walk. It's not just about burning energy — it's about exposure to new sights, smells, surfaces, and sounds. A walk gives your dog the chance to experience the world in a way that builds confidence and adaptability. If you live in an area with varied textures like gravel, grass, concrete, or even stairs, all the better. Navigating different environments helps your dog develop physical coordination and mental resilience.

Daily walks are also where *you* develop your leash skills and leadership. Just like there are rules for feeding, there are rules for leash handling, too — and those will come later. For now, let's focus on the **timing, duration, and purpose** of walking during your dog's day.

When your dog is still learning how to walk on a leash, aim for a **maximum of 15 minutes per session**. These early walks are *training*

Part 1

walks — quality over quantity. Getting a calm, structured walk is far more valuable than just going the distance. Trust me! Teaching your 35-pound puppy good leash manners will save you major headaches when that same dog hits 85 pounds and starts lunging down the street.

I recommend **two walks per day**: one in the morning and another in the evening. If you're still using food in your training — whether treats or kibble — try to walk *before* feeding. This way, your dog will be more motivated and more focused on you rather than the distractions outside.

When it comes to dog gear, your **leash** is one of the most important tools in your toolkit. It gives you control, helps you maintain safety, and teaches your dog boundaries. (More on collars, harnesses, and other training tools in the Worksheet and training tools section.) Right now, let's stick to the leashes.

I prefer a **standard 6-foot leash**, ideally made of **leather** for comfort and durability. I like leashes that have **two handles** — one at the end, and one about halfway down. This gives you more control in high-distraction situations or when you need to guide your dog more precisely. If your long-term goal is off-leash reliability, a **lightweight leash** is a good place to start.

Let me be clear about one thing:
Never use a retractable leash.

This is one of my biggest pet peeves when it comes to dog equipment. Retractable leashes are unsafe, prone to mechanical failure, and can cause serious injury to you or your dog. They also send inconsistent signals to your dog because the leash length is always changing. Even the "good" brands wear out, tangle easily, and confuse leash training altogether. Just skip them.

Walking Recap (for Scheduling)

- **Start with 15-minute training walks**, twice daily — one in the morning, one in the evening.
- **Walk before feeding** to enhance focus and food motivation.

- Use a **6-foot leather leash** with **two handles** for better control and safety.
- **Avoid retractable leashes** at all costs.
- Once your dog is trained, you can extend your walking times freely based on your lifestyle and your dog's energy levels.

Whether you're a runner looking to bring your dog along for your morning miles or someone who enjoys a quiet evening stroll before sunset, a well-trained dog can be the perfect walking companion. But remember, **dogs don't come pre-programmed to walk on a leash.** It's a completely unnatural behavior for them. We expect them to follow our pace, ignore distractions, and not pull toward everything exciting — and none of that is automatic.

So, invest the time early on. Teach your dog that the leash is a guide, not a suggestion. Just like I dedicated more time to breaking down feeding rules earlier, I'll give leash training the same attention later with practical exercises and drills. But for now, stick to a consistent schedule and make walking a meaningful part of your dog's day.

Engagement

Let's move right along to the next piece of the puzzle: **engagement**.

I like to think of engagement as *social play*. This is the kind of interaction with your dog that has **no rules**. Let me give you an example: if you're playing fetch, the "rule" is that the dog brings the toy back to you. That's structured play and a form of enrichment. But **engagement** is different. Engagement is just a *fun*, spontaneous connection between you and your dog. It's you running around and letting your dog chase you. It's calling their name in a silly voice, making fun sounds, and baby-talking just to get their attention. It's giving affection for no reason, just because.

Engagement is about bonding, plain and simple.

Science has shown that the human-canine connection benefits both species. Petting or playing with your dog releases **oxytocin**, the "love hormone," in your brain and theirs. So, while having a dog can be a lot of work, with all the training, feeding, and walking, it also brings serious benefits to your health and happiness.

That's why I say: **don't skip this part** of the day.

It's okay to get down on the floor, roll around, and just have a good time with your dog. I wrestle with my dogs all the time. I engage with them physically, talk to them, and let go of the structured mindset. I'm talking about getting down on all fours, rolling around, getting silly, the whole nine yards. It's fun, and more importantly, it builds **trust**. Just like with feeding, this is one of the daily activities I never recommend skipping. Take your dog to a big field and just run around with them. Let's go off the to-do list for a little while.

We live in a world obsessed with capturing moments, so why not take some selfies with your dog? Find out what goofy sounds make them tilt their head. Massage their ears, rub their paws, and tug on their tail (gently!). All these little moments matter. Bonus: your **groomer will thank you** later when your dog is already used to being touched in these sensitive areas.

As your dog becomes more comfortable with you, your bond will deepen, and with that bond, training will improve exponentially. I've worked with plenty of dogs who do okay with me, but they *thrive* with their favorite person in the family. And guess who that usually is? Not the one who feeds, trains, and manages the schedule. It's often the **teenager** the one who lets the dog sleep in their bed, sneaks them snacks, and plays with them just for fun. That emotional connection matters.

So, I recommend spending **30 minutes twice a day** in simple, no-pressure engagement with your dog. Laugh, play, roll around. Let yourself be a kid again. Think of it as **canine therapy;** the laundry, emails, and chores will still be there when you're done.

Part 1

A Note on Engagement vs. Socialization

There are two schools of thought when it comes to **socializing** a dog.

One approach says that socialization means taking your dog out, letting strangers pet them, giving them treats, and allowing free play with other dogs. The second approach focuses on *engagement,* where your dog is exposed to the outside world but remains **focused on you**, ignoring distractions like other people, animals, or sounds.

I lean more toward the second school of thought.

When I go to the park or a public area where dogs are allowed, I might do a training or engagement session, but I'll often decline when people ask to pet or treat my dog. That's not because I don't want my dog to be friendly, it's because I want my dog to understand that **good things come from their handler**, not from random strangers. A dog that expects treats or affection from everyone can easily become distracted, overstimulated, or even confused about who's in charge.

Let's take a moment to **define what a well-socialized dog is**:

A socialized dog has appropriate behaviors when interacting with other dogs, humans, and especially children. A socialized dog has been exposed to a wide variety of experiences: different surfaces, noises, smells, and environments. They don't react with fear or aggression because they've learned to process the world calmly and confidently.

In this book, I'll sometimes refer to that as a **solid dog** one that's grounded, confident, and well-adjusted. That doesn't happen by accident. It happens through engagement, exposure, and consistent leadership.

Training

And now, we've arrived at the final piece of the puzzle: **training**.

We've already talked about walks, play, and engagement, and yes, all of those are a form of training too. But this part of the day is when we focus specifically on teaching new behaviors and refining existing ones. It's where we step into the realm of structured, deliberate learning, which is often called **behavior modification**.

We'll dive deeper into the nuts and bolts of training later in the book, much like we will do with walks. For now, I want to give you a clear picture of how training fits into your dog's **daily routine**.

Think of training the same way you'd think of any learning process. We all head to school, college, or professional development to pick up new skills. However, gives us too much to learn all at once; suddenly, our brains are buffering like a slow internet connection. We get overloaded, distracted, and tired. The same applies to your dog.

So, when it comes to training, the key is to **keep it short and simple**. The structure I use is called **K.I.S.S.:** *Keep It Simple, Stupid*. It's a funny phrase, but there's truth in it. In my experience, both as a trainer and as a dog owner, simple sessions are the most effective.

I often refer to something I call **"hitting the wall,"** which is when my dog is no longer absorbing anything new. It's a clear sign that it's time to end the session. That's why I generally keep training for **about 15 minutes**. Any longer, and I risk losing focus and progress. Once your dog learns a behavior, it becomes part of your daily routine, something you reinforce naturally throughout the day.

So, remember:

- Training is how we teach or modify behavior.
- Once learned, we **proof** it, which means testing the behavior under different conditions.
- And once it's solid? We just **use it;** no need to overtrain what your dog already knows.

Part 1

Structure of a Training Session

Just like every other part of your dog's life, **structure is everything**.

Here's how I format my training sessions. This structure is especially helpful when teaching a new command, though it also forms the foundation for maintaining or advancing skills in dogs that already have some training on board.

Each session has **three parts**:

1. **Engagement Phase**
2. **Training Phase**
3. **Ending Phase**

1. Engagement Phase

This is how you *start* your training session by getting your dog's attention.

Before you ask for anything, you want to connect. I usually start with a quick engagement game, like the **Name Game** or a little social play. It sets the tone, builds energy, and primes your dog to focus on you. This part only lasts **2–3 minutes**.

It's also important to choose your environment wisely. Don't expect your dog to focus if you're training in a place that's too stimulating, like a dog park or near a busy playground, unless they're already advanced. **Set your dog up for success** by controlling the space as much as possible.

2. Training Phase

This is the core of your session where you teach.

Stick to **one or two new skills** per session. Keep things clear, consistent, and positive. I spend about **10 minutes** here, depending on how my dog responds.

Part 1

Be mindful of your:

- **Body language** — your dog is always reading your posture and movements.
- **Voice and tone** — consistency helps avoid confusion.
- **Rewards** — use whatever motivates your dog most (treats, praise, play, etc.).

Dogs are great observers. Sometimes it's not just the command they're responding to, it's the unintentional cues you're giving through your body language.

3. Ending Phase

Always end on a **win**.

I want my dog to finish every session feeling successful. If the session was challenging, I make sure the last command is something easy, like a '*sit*' or a *name recognition,* something they can do with confidence. That way, the final impression is positive and motivating.

As your dog progresses and begins to master commands, your sessions will evolve. Training then becomes more about **proofing and practicing** skills under different levels of distraction and difficulty. You'll build up complexity over time, but the structure of the session stays largely the same.

There are countless methods and techniques out there, and I'll explore those in greater detail later in this book. But no matter what the approach is, the goal is always the same: clear communication, consistent structure, and a strong bond between human and dog.

The 3 Ds of Dog Training

One of the core concepts we'll come back to again and again in this book is something called the **3 Ds of dog training**: **distance, distraction, and duration**. These are the three factors that most often affect whether your dog follows a command, and understanding them is key to reliable behavior. A lot of people think their dog "knows" a command, but when asked to perform it in a new environment or under different conditions, the dog suddenly doesn't respond. That's not defiance, it's a lack of clarity. Training a behavior isn't just about teaching the dog what to do; it's about helping them understand how to do it anywhere, with anything going on, and for as long as you ask. That's where the 3 D's come in. Let's break each one down.

Distraction

Distraction refers to **anything competing for your dog's attention** people, other dogs, sounds, smells, animals, and even flapping trash bags. Anything.

This is a great place to introduce the concept of your dog's **threshold,** the point at which your dog becomes too overstimulated to listen or focus. A dog's threshold depends on the stimulus. For example, your dog might be okay with balloons around 15 feet away, but loses focus if one comes within 5 feet.

Every dog is different, and **thresholds vary** between stimuli. The good news is you can **work to reduce that threshold** through consistent training. Just make sure you're progressing at your dog's pace and, when in doubt, consult a professional trainer to do this safely, especially if reactivity is involved.

Distance

Distance in dog training refers to **how far away you can be from your dog while still expecting compliance with a command**.

Here's an example: Fido knows how to sit, at least he does when you're three feet away. But what happens if you're across the room, or six feet away? You tell him to sit, and... nothing. Most people assume the dog didn't hear them or got distracted. But really, you may have never trained that command with distance.

This is a classic example of **not testing behavior under different conditions**, which is a key part of proofing — more on that later. But for now, know this: If you haven't practiced the behavior at various distances, your dog probably doesn't fully understand it yet.

Duration

The last D is duration, **how long your dog can maintain the command**.

Let's say you ask your dog to sit. Do they pop back up right away, or can they hold that *'sit'* for 10, 20, or 30 seconds? The same goes for stay, place, or down. How long can your dog hold the behavior?

This one takes patience and repetition, and it improves as your dog gains confidence and clarity in what you're asking.

All three D's **distraction, distance, and duration** are essential to a well-rounded training plan. They can all be improved with consistent practice. That's why **training is a lifelong commitment**. Just like people, dogs need continued learning and reinforcement to maintain and strengthen their skills.

Training Your Dog

So, how often should you train your dog?

At a **minimum,** I recommend training **four times a day for 15 minutes**. As your dog learns more commands and behaviors, you can start mixing things up. Add variety, layer in games, and keep it fun.

For example:

- Once your dog knows how to sit, lay down, and stand on cue, you can play a doggie version of **Simon Says**.

- Try **recall hide-and-seek**. This game is great for building engagement and response to recall. It works best with two people (but you can do it solo if your dog has a reliable wait). The first person calls the dog, then, when the dog arrives, the second person calls the dog. The first person changes location and calls the dog to them. Now the dog must find them. It turns training into a game and builds strong, happy recall.

Part 1

The more you **tap into your dog's instincts and personality**, the better your results will be. And the more you **turn training into play**, the more likely you are to keep up with it. If it's fun for you, it won't feel like a chore.

I'll share more of my favorite training games in the *Worksheets and Tools* section. But with this, we've now completed the breakdown of the **five pillars** of a dog's day, all essential parts of caring for and understanding your dog:

1. Feeding

2. Enrichment

3. Walking

4. Engagement

5. Training

These daily activities are key to maintaining a well-balanced, well-cared-for, and **happy dog**.

Of course, I didn't dive deep into things like **veterinary care** or **grooming** here — not because they aren't important (they're critical), but because they're the obvious parts of dog ownership. This book is about helping you understand the parts of your dog's day that are often overlooked, underutilized, or underappreciated — and how to make the most of them.

Let's take a moment to recap how it all begins when you bring a new dog into your home. Maybe you did your research on breeds, or maybe you didn't. Either way, you've brought your dog home, talked with your family about the house rules, and now you're ready to begin the training journey. Some of you may choose to train your dog independently, while others may seek professional guidance. Regardless of your approach, there are five core elements—what I call the **5 Pillars**—that will naturally be a part of your dog's daily life. These include feeding, walking, enrichment, engagement, and training.

I've outlined each activity below, along with the approximate amount of time you should dedicate to it. Altogether, these add up to about **five**

hours a day. That might sound like a lot, but in my professional opinion, it's the minimum investment of time to provide a well-rounded, fulfilling life for your dog. There's always room to go beyond the minimum—extra time spent on enrichment, engagement, or training only strengthens your bond and builds a more reliable companion.

At the end of the day, most people begin the journey of dog ownership with good intentions—to love and care for their dog. And we should. Dogs have improved the lives of humans for generations. They work as therapy animals, assist in rehabilitation, detect illnesses, and help keep us safe through search-and-rescue or law enforcement work. We owe it to them to give back: that extra belly rub, that extra game of fetch, and yes, that extra bit of training that might one day save their life.

Always remember—there are no good or bad dogs. Only dogs who have or haven't been taught appropriate behaviors.

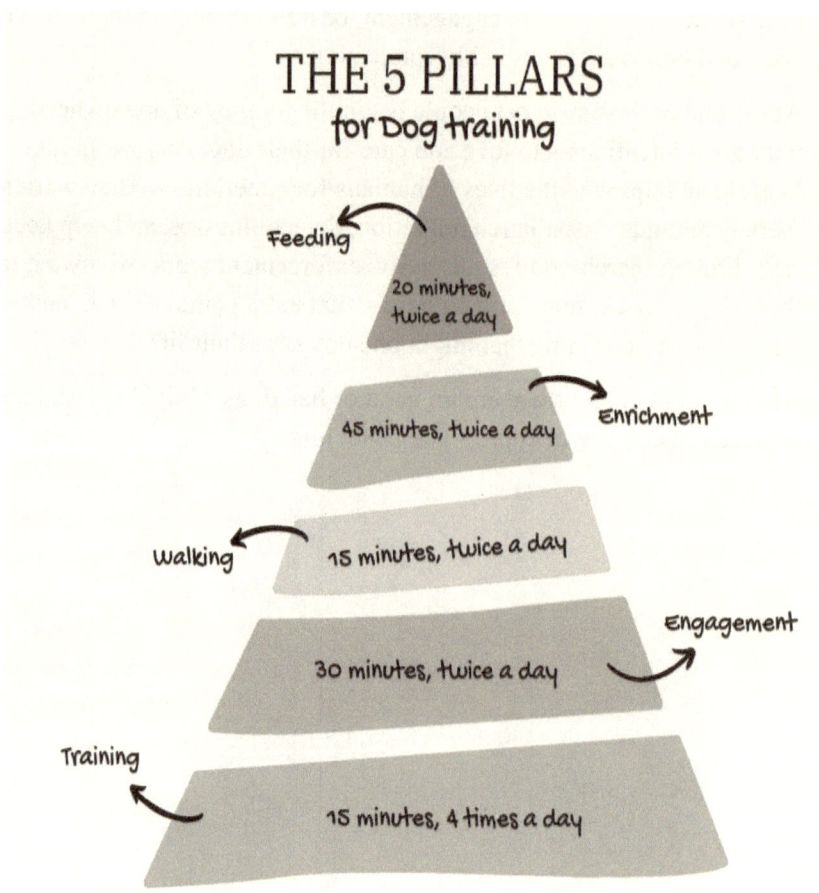

Part 1

Onyx and Omni, My Greatest Teachers

I learned a lot from my dogs. I learned more from working with my dogs than I did from all the books, YouTube, and masterclass instructional videos I'd seen. Some of the things I learned were simple, like the importance of a crate or "dog" proofing your home (and car). Some lessons were obvious, and any logical person would have connected the dots. However, experience is the best teacher, and I will say that I learned some hard lessons. Now I want to share some of these stories to make the point that I made mistakes, but from those, I got better.

Tales of Onyx

As you know, I got Onyx first, and she was the alpha of the pack. I will start with her and the things I learned. Some of these stories are downright embarrassing but worth telling. When I got Onyx, I thought she was incredible, again, "honeymoon stage." The first day she came into my one-bedroom apartment, she was comfortable. She walked around the perimeter and checked things out. She seemed at home. This was a nice moment for me. It confirmed my decision to spend the last of my money on this dog.

The first night, she slept through the night and didn't make a peep. She slept in the crate, and it was great. Because of all the horror stories I'd heard about dogs, I thought I'd won the lottery with this dog. After about a week, I needed to get more dog supplies, and I thought taking her would be a great idea.

Surprise! Reactivity on Aisle 3

This was my first lesson in dog reactivity. I didn't realize at that point that Onyx had this behavioral issue. As I looked through the bins of toys, a dog at the far end of the store crossed the aisle. Onyx caught a glimpse and instantly exploded in barking. Until that moment, I hadn't heard her bark, so it completely blindsided me. She was only 10 pounds, but she was *loud* and *wild*. I had no idea what to do, so I did the only thing I could: I took her outside.

💡 *Lesson: Training doesn't always start when you say "sit." Sometimes it starts when you're standing embarrassed, smack in the middle of a pet store, wondering what just happened.*

She would get into the window of my living room and bark at dogs passing. She would do this in the car when dogs went by or if we drove by dogs. It was embarrassing every single time. Through this experience, though, I learned about desensitization training. How to slowly expose my dog to stimuli that I want them to ignore. As I worked with my mentor, who was just my dog trainer at the time, she got better. She learned invaluable skills.

Potty Training, Protest Pees, and... the Driver's Seat Incident

Onyx was mostly great at potty training. She was likely older than I thought when I got her, which helped. But she taught me some lessons that no book ever mentioned.

She had a habit of **submissive and excited peeing**. No matter how gentle or soft-spoken someone was, she'd leak a little every time she got scared or overly excited. Worse, she'd wag her tail and *fan the pee around the room*. Not ideal.

Then came one of the most embarrassing moments of all: I left her in the car with some leftover food tucked under the seat. Rookie mistake. Not only did she eat the food, but she also **peed all over my driver's seat**. My car reeked until the day I sold it.

Later, when I brought home Omni, Onyx wasn't happy. In protest, she **peed on my bed**. Message received.

Lesson: Dogs communicate in their own way. Be ready to listen—even if it means changing your sheets

The Little Dog with a Big Dog Heart

Onyx was fearless. She was my demo dog for training clients, my hiking and camping companion, and even learned agility. She helped teach Omni the ropes and had this "big dog" mindset wrapped in a tiny 12-pound frame. I couldn't have asked for a better first dog to teach me how to be a dog trainer.

Tales of Omni

Omni came into my life less than a year after Onyx, as a birthday present to myself. She was a shepherd mix, just a little pup who could walk under Onyx at first. But by the time she was fully grown, Onyx could walk under her.

Puppy Mayhem and the Voice Recorder Incident

Omni was around 6–8 weeks old when I got her, and she taught me everything I didn't know about **puppy development**.

She peed constantly. I was taking her out every hour, and it still felt like she'd sneak in a "surprise" right after coming back inside. The nights were especially tough. The lack of sleep, the frustration, the mess—I questioned whether I was cut out for this.

She chewed everything: cords, furniture, shoes, clothes, even a voice recorder filled with personal notes and ideas. That one hurt.

Lesson: Puppy-proof your home. Seriously. If it's within reach, it's fair game.

Part 1

Progress Isn't Linear

One of the biggest lessons Omni taught me was that **training isn't a straight path**. I remember working with her for what felt like forever and still feeling like I was failing. She pulled on walks, barked at everything, ignored commands, and had no concept of "stay." For a long time, I didn't like her. I even questioned whether I should be a trainer at all.

But I kept at it.

One day, sometime after her third birthday, I noticed a shift. We were training at home, running through a series of commands, and she crushed it. Then we went to a group class with my mentor, and she was laser focused. She worked like a dream. Suddenly, I realized: all those frustrating, seemingly fruitless training sessions had built something solid.

🔑 *Lesson: Just because you can't see progress doesn't mean it's not happening. Trust the process.*

Canine Christmas and Mystery Mayhem

Of course, not all lessons were profound. Like the time I learned never to leave Christmas presents under the tree. One of my dogs destroyed every gift—tore up wrapping paper, ruined boxes, and even **ripped giant holes in my sofa**. And no, it wasn't Omni. It was Onyx. Somehow, that little terrier went full wrecking ball while I was out.

To this day, I don't know how she did it.

Reflection

Working with Onyx and Omni taught me more about dogs—and myself—than any book ever could. They were my first real teachers in dog training. They made me better through the mess, the mistakes, and the moments of doubt. Trust wasn't built in a single session. It was built through showing up every day, consistently, even when I didn't feel like it.

That's the foundation this book is built on.

Training Has Already Started

One of the biggest misconceptions in dog training is the idea that training begins when the leash comes out, or when the owner decides it's time. Training starts long before that. It begins the moment your dog meets you, whether it's at a shelter, a breeder, or through a friend. Every interaction you have is part of the learning process.

Dogs are constantly observing, adjusting, and learning. The problem is, they don't wait for a training session to start picking up on cues. They don't know the difference between "training time" and "real life." To them, it's all the same. Which means whether you know it or not, you're already training them.

Part 1

Onyx: My First Lesson in Unintentional Training

When I met Onyx at that PetSmart event in Yuba City, California, I had no idea what I was really getting into. I wanted a dog more than anything, but I didn't understand yet how much I was already teaching her just by how I behaved. She was in the shelter system, already learning things about people, routines, and expectations. Shelter dogs are learning from every person who walks by their kennel. Some learn that barking gets attention. Others learn that staying quiet gets them overlooked.

Onyx was confident, alert, and independent. That was clear from the first moment I saw her. But what wasn't clear to me then was that I was shaping her behavior from day one. If I had nervously approached her with treats, she would have learned I was soft. If I let her pull ahead on the leash during that first walk in the parking lot, she would have learned she could lead me. These aren't formal lessons, but they would still be lessons. She was watching, analyzing, and storing information away for later.

When we got home, I had no structured plan, just a heart full of love and a bag of food. I let her roam the apartment, sniff everything, and climb on furniture. I thought I was giving her freedom and showing her, she was safe. What I was really doing was teaching her that this space was hers to do with as she pleased. It took months of unlearning and redirecting those early behaviors because I didn't know that training had already started.

 Bringing Onyx home that day wasn't just the beginning of our life together; it was the start of shaping how she would understand and engage with the human world. I remember getting her home, watching her sniff every corner of the small apartment, tail high and ears alert. I was excited and nervous. Just a crate. No plan. Just vibes and a couple of YouTube videos under my belt. I thought I had time to figure it out. But the truth was—training had already begun.

She jumped on the couch. I let it slide. She barked at the neighbor's dog through the window. I laughed. She pawed at my legs while I made food. I handed her a scrap. In just the first few hours, I unknowingly set the tone for behaviors that would take me months to adjust.

Part 1

Omni: Day One Mistakes and Miracles

With Omni, things were a little different. She came into my life when I had more experience, and that changed everything. She was my first puppy, from day one. The contrast between her upbringing and Onyx's was night and day. I remember picking her up and her falling asleep in my lap on the ride home. Pure innocence. But puppies aren't exactly blank slates. She had already learned something about the world in her first few weeks, most of it revolving around survival instincts, curiosity, and energy.

Omni was a different kind of challenge. Unlike Onyx, who was adopted as a young adult, Omni was a puppy. That meant her slate was still relatively clean, but it also meant every decision I made mattered tenfold. The moment I picked her up and put her in the car, she started learning. She learned how I handled stress, how I responded to her whining, and how I carried myself.

The first night with Omni, I thought crate training would be a breeze because Onyx did so well. I was wrong. She whined and barked almost the entire night. Well, the times she didn't were when I took her outside to potty, most of which was just spent staring at one another. That night, I unintentionally set the precedent for bedtime routine and communication. For weeks after, getting her to sleep in a crate was a battle. Why? I taught her that whining meant freedom, anytime she wanted. I just hadn't realized it.

One of my earliest challenges with Omni was managing her frustration tolerance. As a puppy, she would cry when confined, even for a minute. I remember sitting next to her crate the first night, just outside the bars like a prison buddy, whispering encouragement to her. Over time, I began shaping positive crate associations. Her meals were fed in the crate. Treats only came when she voluntarily went in. And I never used the crate as punishment. By the time she was six months old, she would sprint into her crate the moment I said, "Kennel."

I remember walking into the kitchen one morning and finding her sitting politely, staring up at the counter where she had seen me prepare her food the day before. She wasn't barking. She wasn't jumping. She was just sitting, waiting. She had already begun learning patterns. In just 24 hours, Omni had started picking up on my routines and expectations, even though I hadn't formally taught them.

I often share these moments with clients to show that training doesn't start with a command—it starts with awareness. If your dog pulls toward people on a leash, and you move closer, that's training. If they jump, and you give them attention, training. If they bark and you respond, you're reinforcing barking.

Your Dog is Learning Even When You're Not Teaching

This is the cornerstone of effective training: **your dog is always learning.** Whether you're at the park, on the couch, or taking a phone call, your dog is gathering data. They're watching where you put your keys, how you talk to strangers, how you react when they bark, and what earns them a smile, a frown, or a treat.

It doesn't matter if your dog is six weeks old or six years old. From the moment they arrive, they're being trained. That's why consistency, structure, and awareness matter so much. You don't have to be perfect, but you do need to be intentional.

Action Steps for New Owners:

1. **Start with Structure**: From the first day home, set boundaries. Decide where your dog is allowed to go, where they sleep, and how feeding times work.

2. **Watch Your Reactions**: Are you reinforcing jumping by giving attention? Are you encouraging begging by feeding from the table?

3. **Build a Routine**: Dogs thrive on consistency. Feed, walk, and train the same each day.

4. **Reward What You Like**: Catch your dog doing the right thing and reward it. Sitting quietly? Reward. Waiting at the door? Reward. Eye contact? Reward.

5. **Understand the Power of Silence**: Sometimes what you don't respond to is just as powerful as what you do. Ignore behaviors you don't want to encourage.

So, if you're wondering when to start training your dog, here's the answer: you already have. The moment your dog saw you, sniffed you, or heard your voice, the learning began. Your job now is to steer that learning in the right direction. Be consistent. Be fair. Be aware.

Training isn't just what you do in 10-minute sessions with treats in your pocket. It's who you are with your dog, every minute of the day.

Onyx and Omni taught me that lesson in very different ways. And now, I'm passing it on to you.

Let's get intentional, because the training has already started.

Now, this isn't to say everything needs to be perfect from day one. It's not about perfection, it's about intention. The moment your dog is observing you, they're learning. They're picking up on your habits, your boundaries, your tolerance, and your energy. You don't need to run a military camp, but you do need a plan.

This is why I say: **The training has already started.** It started the moment you saw your dog. It continued when you signed the adoption papers, and it hit full stride when you opened the car door and brought them home.

What makes this phase so important is that it sets the tone for everything else. I call this the *Foundational Phase*. It's where your dog learns what's expected, what's acceptable, and how to find safety and structure in a brand-new environment.

Key Lessons from Onyx & Omni

*   **Onyx's Door Bolting Phase**: For the first few weeks, Onyx would sprint out the front door if I wasn't paying attention. I treated it like a game—she treated it like a challenge. Eventually, I began to reinforce a solid "wait" at the door and later taught a reliable recall. This problem didn't go away overnight, but it

taught me to stop reacting emotionally and start creating structured responses.

- **Omni's Jumping Habit**: As a high-energy shepherd mix, Omni wanted to greet everyone. Jumping was her love language. The problem was, not everyone appreciated a 60-pound fur missile to the chest. I started redirecting her energy into a "sit for pets" routine. Every guest was instructed to ignore her unless she had all four paws on the ground. Within a couple of weeks, I had a polite greeter.

Pro Tip:

Shelter Dogs Often Arrive Pre-Trained... Just Not the Way You Think.

Many shelter dogs have learned to be pushy, self-reliant, or even shut down emotionally. That's not their fault, it's how they've survived. When you adopt, you don't just start from zero. You're often unpacking habits that were created out of necessity. Be patient. Be consistent. And remember, day one matters.

Part 2:

Now Dog Training Can Start

Part 2

Essential vs Non-Essential Commands

In the first part of this book, we covered some great topics to start you off on the best paw with your new dog or maybe reestablish some new behaviors with an existing dog. Now let's get to training. In this portion of the book, I go step by step the "how-to" for training. This will include some of my favorite training drills, exercises, and games. Some of the methods I will briefly explain, while others I might go into more detail. I'll give you a great example, I won't be going over a lot of the puppy training like potty training, crate training, etc. There are tons of great resources available on those subjects, many of which I agree with and don't have anything additional to add.

First, let's discuss the different types of commands that you can teach your dog. I like to break this into two separate categories: **essential vs non-essential commands.** This can be a bit subjective. What I think is important, someone might disagree. This is where you get to handpick what commands are primary and fit the lifestyle you want to live. So, to define them both, **essential commands are behaviors that are universally acceptable or potentially lifesaving.** While **non-essential commands are behaviors that are unnecessary and/or can be defined as trick behavior (i.e., rollover).**

Dog training has been around for approximately 150 years. This means that we have developed many behaviors that we want our dogs to know. But which ones matter and which ones don't? I organize my commands based on whether the behavior is useful or going to ensure the health and safety of not only my dog but also others. "Sit," surprisingly, is a **non-essential** command to me. Sure! Having a dog that can sit on command is great, polite, but it doesn't do much. However, "stay" is an **essential command,** and because of that, I do train my dog to sit, but as a standalone, it's not that important. I have provided my list of **Essential and Non-Essential commands.** I have also included a template for you to develop your list.

Part 2

▶ Get the printable version and demo video:
https://bit.ly/ilikemydogbookresources

Essential Commands

- Stay/wait
- Name
- Drop it
- Leave it
- Let's go or heel
- Recall
- Doorway manners
- Release
- *Sit – when paired with essential*

Non-essential Commands

- Sit
- Shake
- Rollover
- Bark
- Play Dead
- Look at me

Now, I do want to emphasize that this is my list and in no way the industry standard. Some of these you might be scratching your head at, and some of these you might agree with. I do want to add that advanced commands or commands for working dogs are all essential. This includes military, law enforcement, and service dogs, because the work they do could be lifesaving.

In this section, I will give a general framework for teaching any command. This will be the general process I use when it comes to teaching a new behavior. I will also go through the step-by-step process of how to teach *"Primary commands all dogs should know."*

Part 2

New Dog, Old Dog, Same Tricks?

Anyone can train a dog. It only takes consistency, patience, and a bit of behavioral science. Dog training comes down to good habits and reinforcement of desired behaviors. I won't go into operant training now but just remember that 'positive' means to add and 'negative' means to remove. So, punishment and reward don't need to be defined, but when training, picking which method will increase or decrease the frequency of a command is important.

I will cover some methods and terms before going into the process of teaching "New Behaviors." There are many different methods of training, but I'm going to go over the foundational trio of training, which in whole or some part is used by all training styles. Training styles are defined as a much broader approach to training that differs based on methods, philosophy, tools, and approach to dog training. I won't be going into styles at all in this book.

Methods of learning

The foundational trio of training, as I like to call them, are the keystones that all methods are built on in some form or fashion. When you think about training your dog, no matter what style you might lean towards, the foundational trio is being used. This includes Luring, Shaping, and Capturing. I might have mentioned them at some point already, but I want to define them and dive deeper into how to use them.

Foundational Trio

1. Luring – This method uses a toy or treat to guide your dog into a desired behavior.

How it works:

You move the toy or reward in a way that encourages the dog to follow it with its nose. As they do this, their body naturally moves into the position you want (e.g. sitting).

Part 2

Example:

Teaching 'sit,' hold a treat close to your dog's nose and slowly move it up and back over their head. Their heads go up, and butt goes down, due to body mechanics.

2. Capturing – this method is waiting for your dog to do some desired behavior naturally, then you mark and reward it.

How it works:

You don't prompt or guide, just observe and reward. When the dog does the behavior a few times, they will connect the behavior with the reward.

Example:

When your dog lies down, you mark and reward them. Do this consistently and your dog will start to lay more to earn rewards

3. Shaping – This method is used to teach complex behaviors by rewarding smaller behaviors that progress to the overall behavior.

How it works:

You reward simple behaviors that gradually require more from the dog over time.

Example:

Teaching a dog to ring a bell. Start with simple behaviors and progress to the more complex.

- Reward for looking at the bell
- Reward sniffing the bell
- Reward any touching of the bell
- Reward for ringing the bell

Now that we have that added to our toolbox of dog training, let's talk about the ways we communicate with our dogs. This is done through our words but largely through our body language. Dogs learn hand commands for behaviors, but they are also associating the subtleties in your body language, some of which you might not know that you are doing. So, when you are prompting a sit or stay, be conscience of the body language. The more consistent you are with your body language, the clearer your communication and the less chance for miscommunication. Let me provide an example about what might cause some confusion. Let's say you are working on teaching your dog a solid 'stay' command, and when you 'release' you gesture in towards your body and drop your hand to your side. Now, when you prompt the dog to 'sit' after giving the hand command, you drop your hand to your side, and your dog gets up. This is because your dog has associated dropping your hand with 'release.'

This brings me to Rule #2: The Rule of **ONE**. This is a very crucial component of dog training concerning communication with your dog. It's broken into three different parts, one command per one behavior. If you teach your dog to lie down, don't say 'lay' in some scenarios and 'down' in others. This is a great house rules topic, making sure everyone in the house is saying the same command. Second, say it one time, never repeat yourself. We want to make sure that the dog associates 'sit' with the behavior, not 'sit, sit' pause 'sit' and for good measure 'sit.' So, say it once and get the behavior, not four times or some ambiguous number of times. The last component, you have one second to reinforce a behavior. You prompt your dog to 'sit,' and you get distracted by a text or doing something else. Your dog sees a bird and decides to chase after it and has forgotten about the 'sit.' Maybe you reward them just before they run off. Maybe when the dog runs back to you, you reward the dog, but now they associate it with something other than the 'sit.' So, mark the right behavior within one second.

Rule #2: The Rule of One

- One command per one behavior
- Never repeat yourself, say it once
- One second to reinforce, mark the behavior

That covers just how simple it is to communicate with your dog. Now that we have covered those standards, we can move into the marker words. This is how we verbally communicate to our dogs what behaviors we like or dislike. If you pair the marker with the right positive or negative condition, you have a fully developed communication system with your dog. Just short of leash communication, you are 85% there. Below, I have included the marker words with their meanings.

Marker Words

1. Positive – This marker (often the word "yes" or the sound of a clicker) comes immediately after the desired behavior and before the reward. It tells the dog that the correct behavior has been performed, and when followed by a reward, it creates a clear association through positive reinforcement.
2. Negative—This marker is usually "No" and can often be overused. This is why I suggest something a bit more uncommon, like a buzzer sound you won't use in conversation, so you don't confuse your dog when you are not talking to them. Remember, they are always observing you. This marks that the behavior that preceded was undesired, and when paired with positive/negative punishment, it will decrease the behavior.
3. Neutral – This marker is usually **"good,"** which comes during a continuing command, like loose leash walking or a hold. This can be paired with a reward, but typically doesn't have to be, it communicates to the dog that the behavior you are doing, I like, so keep doing it.
4. Release – This marker is usually **"release,"** which comes at the end of any behavior, like a stay/wait command. This communicates that the command is done, so your dog can go back to doing whatever they want. I know some people like to use *"okay,"* again, that's a word that is commonly used in everyday conversation and can pose some confusion. So, please try not to use that one for your release word.

That just about does it. We have our marker words and commands, we understand the methods needed to teach a command, so now we are just about ready to start training. First, let's briefly talk about the training tools that you will need at a minimum. There are tons of different training aids,

Part 2

tools, and rewards, so this again is an aspect that is highly individualized per the dog or goal. This list is the essential training starter kit, in my opinion.

Training essentials

1. *Leash* – lightweight and durable 6 ft lead.

2. *Rewards* – this can vary from food, toys, to attention.
3. *Longline*- lightweight and durable 15 ft, 20 ft, or 30 ft line.
4. *Treat Pouch* – something that has separate pockets to divide different values of treats recommended.
5. *Cot/bed* – a lightweight, portable cot or mat that can be transported with you from location to location.

That is about all you need to get some good training started. Sure, you will want to get other things, like once your dog has some foundational training done, an e-collar. I love using a heel stick for training, just to name one of several training aids available. I highly recommend researching the specific training tools needed for specific behaviors. Now that we have covered methods, communication, and training tools, we can start with the general outline of training. This is the barebones structure and process of training for any command. While there might be minor differences in space or tools needed, this is a great ground-level start to all commands.

Training Process

First, let's discuss the structure of training and how to be successful with each session. The biggest component of training is consistency. Remember that training isn't linear, but over time, the hard work will pay off. This doesn't just mean having a schedule for training but also making sure to do everything consistently in your dog's life. If you have your dog 'sit' before every meal, that becomes standard. Never train when frustrated. I will repeat that one: **Never train when frustrated.** It will happen, it happens to me regrettably, and thankfully, I have great people, like my partner, to help reel me in when my judgment is cloudy. Dogs don't understand emotions. They understand that when you are in a heightened state that it's confusing and potentially scary. If your dog is anxious or scared, they are not learning what you want them to learn. So, to control your dog, first you must control yourself.

The structure of training is also particularly important. I keep the sessions short and intentional, as discussed in the previous section. The length of training should not exceed 20 minutes; you will get more out of several short sessions than longer, dense sessions. Also, having three levels (low, medium, high) of rewards will come in handy. This is to help vary the reward system but also have something to compete with various levels of distractions that might bid for your dog's attention. The last thing before you start training is setting your goal for the session. Having a clear objective can make all the difference. Refer to the Structure of Training Sessions about the three separate phases of training.

General Training Overview:

Training starts in a non-distraction environment on leash. We start with some social play and easy focus drills like the name game. This typically lasts for 2 to 3 minutes of the session, just to prime your dog to focus and listen to instructions. The training phase starts with focusing on one or two behaviors max per session, using whichever method is most effective. For example, using luring for sitting or shaping for more complex behavior. If the dog doesn't know the command at all, start with only the hand command. Mark the desired behavior with 'yes,' reward, and repeat. I don't say the word until my dog understands the hand command well, and then I pair the verbal cue to the behavior. This typically will take several sessions of progression. Be creative with drills, reward frequency, and location. This part must be fun for both you and the dog. If the training isn't fun, no one benefits from it. After, we move to the end phase, which is just ending the session on a positive note of something your dog is good at, so they have a positive association. I try to have my sessions very relaxed and casual to mimic my normal day. I like to do sessions at all different times throughout the day. This way, my dog doesn't associate good behavior only with training sessions. Now we rinse and repeat until

Part 2

we are getting a success rate with both verbal and hand commands. This means 80% proficiency when prompting a command.

Below, I have provided a general training worksheet to use with examples of how to teach a new command.

🐾 *General Training Session Worksheet*

Use this worksheet to structure and track your daily training sessions. The goal is to ensure consistency, progress, and fun throughout your training journey.

✅ Session Overview

Date: _____
Location: _____
Time of Day: _____
Distraction Level: ☐ None ☐ Low ☐ Medium ☐ High

🎯 Warm-Up (2–3 min)

Use light social play and a focus drill (like the name game) to prime your dog.

What activity did you use to engage your dog?

Dog's engagement level: ☐ Low ☐ Medium ☐ High

🎓 Training Focus

Focus on 1–2 behaviors max per session. Choose the most effective method (luring, shaping, or capturing).

Part 2

Behavior 1: _____

Training Method Used: ☐ Luring ☐ Shaping ☐ Capturing

Starting with Hand Command Only? ☐ Yes ☐ No

Progress Notes (include success rate, challenges, and wins):

_____

_____

Behavior 2 (optional): _____

Training Method Used: ☐ Luring ☐ Shaping ☐ Capturing

Starting with Hand Command Only? ☐ Yes ☐ No

Progress Notes:

_____

_____

💬 Cue Progression

Once your dog reliably performs the behavior with the hand signal, pair the verbal cue.

Has a verbal cue been introduced yet? ☐ Yes ☐ No

If yes, what is the cue? _____

Observed proficiency (aim for 80%):

☐ Below 50% ☐ 50–70% ☐ 70–80% ☐ Above 80%

_____

_____

🫀 End on a Positive

Wrap up the session with a behavior your dog already knows and enjoys.

Which behavior was used to end the session?

_____

_____

Part 2

Dog's mood at end of session: ☐ Relaxed ☐ Excited ☐ Frustrated ☐ Tired

---

Notes & Reflections

What went well? What can be improved next session?

Modifying and Refining Behaviors

This next topic is basically "troubleshooting" behaviors. As we know, when learning or working with your dog, this is often far less likely to be ideal. This is why training is a lifelong journey and not a destination. Your dog will pick up habits; you might teach things the wrong way, trust me, I've done it. Or more likely, you get a dog with some behavioral problems. So, let's figure out how to deal with those issues.

Modifying behaviors

In the most general sense, modifying behaviors can be defined as changes and/or complete removal of existing behaviors. This could be as simple as your dog jumping on you when greeting you, working through anxiety, or barking. Always consult professional dog trainers when dealing with advanced behavior modification. In most cases, there is some disconnect between behavior and expectation. This could be due to improper training or progressing faster than the dog's understanding. The simplest solution is going back to the basics and retraining the behavior from square one. Minor changes in timing your reward, marker, or lowering the

Part 2

requirement of the behavior might need to be done. I will provide two different examples to compare and highlight how one might troubleshoot.

Scenario 1:

In this example, Rick has a dog that he has been working on, "sit' and lay.' However, when Rick notices that every time he prompts for a 'sit', within a few seconds, his dog lies down. How can Rick fix this problem?

Solution:

This is a very minor issue; however, if you plan on competing with your dog, this can cause some problems. What is happening here? The dog has associated or anticipates the lay prompt after sitting. In most cases, dogs learn the 'lay' command. They are prompted to sit, followed by a 'lay' command. This is a classic case of progressing a bit faster than the dog. In this case, Rick will start to train to lie separately from sitting. Having the dog lie without having to sit first. Also, Rick works on the duration of the sit command and ignoring unprompted 'lay' commands. Rick can also reinforce the 'sit' command sooner.

Scenario 2:

In this example, Rick's dog charges the door when he gets home and greets him by jumping on Rick. The dog has almost knocked Rick down before. How can Rick fix this problem?

Solution:

This is a very common problem that happens to a lot of dog owners. This can be solved by several methods. One shortcut is not allowing access by using a crate, by using a partition, or being in the backyard. Not giving the dog an opportunity reduces frequency; however, this is not a solution. The way I would handle this first is by addressing the proper greeting routine, starting with the basics and working up to coming home. This is again going to come with training and timing. The other step is giving the problem a name. So, when Omni jumped, I trained her to do it on command and only prompted the behavior very infrequently. This is a great example of using capturing. Another solution is getting the dog to associate Rick's coming home with waiting on a bed or cot.

Refining Behaviors

Some behaviors are desired but need a bit of polishing. Refining is just helping mold behaviors closer to the ideal. I will cover this in more detail in the proofing section of this book. I wanted to briefly speak on this topic as it relates to modifying and how they differ from one another. As we learned, modifying is a change to an existing behavior that is typically undesired. Refining is defined as small adjustments to existing behaviors for the goal of meeting a behavioral standard. Later, I will discuss the concept of precision, which is a more detailed look into refinement.

Primary Commands all dogs should know

This is the final part of this section. This list is again my list that I have developed over the years as the most important commands that all dogs should know. This is the bare minimum that all my dogs know, and most of the foundational commands that I teach my clients. The way I picked the commands that made this list is based on the criteria below.

Primary Criteria

1. *Command must be in high demand with a high daily frequency*
2. *Command is potentially lifesaving for my dog or others.*
3. *Command helps improve my dog's quality of life*

From the list above, I have created, in no particular order, my top five Primary Commands. While I teach other commands, these are the ones that are the most important. I just can't emphasize that enough. Below is the list of those commands.

▶ Get the printable version and demo video:
https://bit.ly/ilikemydogbookresources

Part 2

Primary Commands

1. ***Recall*** – *dog coming when called to the owner, no matter where or what they are doing*
2. ***Leave it /Drop it*** – *dog breaking focus from a stimulus when prompted, this includes eye contact or picking something up*
3. ***Stay/Wait*** – *dog holding a position and not moving until release ('place' – staying on a designated spot. This can be a cot, bed, or bench).*
4. ***Leash walking*** – *dog walking properly on leash*
5. ***Stop (or Drop)*** – *dog drops into a 'lay' position no matter what they are doing (typically done in route to owner).*

Training "Recall"

This is one of the most important commands. If you have a solid recall, you can save your dog's life. Each command has a start and end, which is crucial in ensuring the dog understands what is being asked and can perform the expected behavior. Recall starts when the dog has committed to coming to you. The command ends when the dog sits in front of you, not just when the dog gets close. During the learning phase, it's important to have the dog sit and get a hand on the dog's collar or leash so that the dog doesn't just run away. This isn't a game of tag after all. I'm going to go through the process of training recall. I will give you two different levels of difficulty so that you can train. You will have a place to start, fill in the middle with your own experience, and adjust the level of difficulty. Once you reach the advanced example, feel free to go beyond that. There are countless scenarios, and I'm sure that I could write an entire book on just recalling alone. However, for the sake of time, I will provide you with enough to get started and something to achieve as you progress.

Recall 101: The Basics

Training Goal: Teach the dog the foundation for the recall command (non-cue session)

Methods: Leash Pressure, shaping, and positive reinforcement

Part 2

Training tools needed: Leash and dog's preferred reward (treats, toys, or tugs)

Training the 'recall' command will always be done in a controlled and enclosed environment for safety. Make sure to minimize or eliminate any distractions that might interfere with the learning phase of this command. As your dog progresses, we will start to introduce more distractions or difficulties at a gradual pace. Once your area is prepped, training can start.

1. Start with social play to get your dog focused and engaged. This consists of having the dog chase you a bit, playing tug, or doing the name game. This is all done while the dog is on a leash. (2 – 3 minutes).

2. Using a standard 6 ft leash with some distance between you and the dog, apply leash pressure by pulling the leash tight enough to encourage the dog to come towards you. Verbal encouragement may be given to help lure the dog towards you. This can be fun, sounds like "pup pup pup," or kissy noises. Once the dog has committed to coming, release pressure and prompt the dog to sit in front of you. (If this is the first session or the dog is unaware of the recall command, don't say the command at this point.)

3. Once the dog is sitting in front of you, mark the behavior with a positive marker and maintain eye contact for about 2 or 3 seconds before delivering a reward. This will set the standard of not coming and immediately running away from you. (3 – 5 minutes)

4. Disengage by walking around a bit and giving your dog the chance to create distance from you. If needed, enlist the help of a second person to get the dog's attention, or have them also do a recall with the same standard to create the distance. (1 – 2 minutes)

5. Repeat steps 3 and 4. Still not prompting the recall. Apply leash pressure, release when the dog is committed to coming, and prompt the sit. Mark the behavior, maintain eye contact, and deliver a reward. (2-3 minutes)

6. End session with a few known commands, like sit, or prompt your dog with their name or look command. (2 minutes)

Part 2

▶ Get the printable version and demo video:
https://bit.ly/ilikemydogbookresources

This is session one and the basic framework for teaching recall. In this session, we are just priming the behavior and building the foundation. I typically will do several sessions without introducing any cue. This is to ensure the dog understands the expected behavior. To ensure success, we control the environment and distractions, effectively time rewards, and use consistent training methods. When applying leash pressure, you should never drag the dog towards you. The leash pressure is a positive punishment, which is turned off when the dog moves toward the force in the direction of the handler. This pressure should never be aggressive or cause discomfort to your dog. The level of pressure shouldn't be so tight that it causes your dog to pull in the opposite direction.

Every dog is unique in their learning style, so remember to be patient. This basic session might take several sessions over a few days to a couple of weeks. Once your dog is responding to the leash pressure immediately, you are ready to introduce the cue.

Recall 101: The Basics

Training Goal: Teach the dog recall command, introducing the cue

Methods: Leash Pressure, shaping, and positive reinforcement

Training tools needed: Leash and dog's preferred reward (treats, toys, or tugs)

Training the 'recall' command will always be done in a controlled and enclosed environment for safety. Make sure to minimize or eliminate any distractions that might interfere with the learning phase of this command. As your dog progresses, we will start to introduce more distractions or difficulties at a gradual pace. Once your area is prepped, training can start.

1. Start with social play to get your dog focused and engaged. This consists of having the dog chase you a bit, playing tug, or doing the name game. This is all done while the dog is on leash. (2 – 3 minutes).

Part 2

2. Using a standard 6 ft leash with some distance between you and the dog, apply leash pressure by pulling the leash tight enough to encourage the dog to come towards you. Verbal encouragement may be given to help lure the dog towards you. This can be fun, sounds like "pup pup pup," or kissy noises. Once the dog has committed to coming, release pressure. Once the dog is about 1 ft away from you, give the recall command. I use "here" for my recall; however, choose something you like that works for your family. Then prompt the dog to sit in front of you.

3. Once the dog is sitting in front of you, mark the behavior with a positive marker and maintain eye contact for about 2 or 3 seconds before delivering a reward. This will set the standard of not coming and immediately running away from you. (3 – 5 minutes) *If needed, it's okay to gently grab the dog's collar underneath the chin to prevent them from running off. I suggest doing this only a few times and quickly fading this away so that the dog doesn't associate being held in place as the end of the recall.

4. Disengage by walking around a bit and give your dog the chance to create distance from you. If needed, enlist the help of a second person to get the dog's attention, or also have them do a recall with the same standard to create the distance. (1 – 2 minutes)

5. Repeat steps 3 and 4. Still prompting recall about 1 ft away from you. (2-3 minutes)

6. End session with a few known commands, like sit, or prompt your dog with a name or look command. (2 minutes)

Lesson: Run away from your dog just a few feet before turning toward them and stopping to encourage them to run towards you. Reward them when they sit in front of you.

This session should be done after achieving a high level of success with the "*Recall Basic 101: Foundation for recall*" is complete. Things to note: Slowly increase the distance that you prompt the dog to do the recall command. This should be done in stages over numerous sessions. The rule of thumb is to start with 20% of your distance and increase in 20% increments until you have 100% working distance. So, for example, using

Part 2

a 10ft line for ease of math. I will follow all the steps above. Once my dog is 2 feet away from me, I will prompt the "recall" command. I will do this over several sessions before moving up to 40% (4 ft), 60% (6 ft), and so on until I reach the full 100% (10 ft).

That is the basic framework for teaching the recall command in an environment with no distractions. This is where the foundation is built. Consistency builds muscle memory and confidence in your dog. When your dog is confused or startled, it will have something to fall back on, like its recall. Some more noteworthy items to mention. Always remember dog training rules. #1: **Never lie to your dog** – regarding the recall command, never call your dog over to punish or correct them. This will cause a negative association with the recall and decrease the willingness to comply. #2: **Rule of ONE** – One command for one behavior, say the command one time and reinforce within one second. I know that I said to maintain eye contact for 2-3 seconds after the dog sits; the positive marker is your verbal reinforcement, which should be given immediately when the dog sits at the end of the recall.

Now, we are going to move to a more advanced setup. I recommend starting with "Recall 101: The Basics" and gradually increasing to this level. This next example should be done after successfully working towards it. It will include real-world distractions and a much higher level of difficulty.

Recall 400: The Advanced Recall Session

Training Goal: Recall Foundation working up to 50 ft away (with low distractions)

Methods: Leash Pressure, shaping, and positive reinforcement

Training tools needed: Leash and dog's preferred reward (treats, toys, or tugs)

Training the 'recall' command will always be done in a controlled, enclosed environment for safety. Make sure to include any distractions

Part 2

that might interfere with the behavior for the training goal. As your dog progresses, we will start to introduce more distractions or difficulties at a gradual pace. Once your area is prepped, training can start.

1. Start with social play to get your dog focused and engaged. This consists of having the dog chase you a bit, playing tug, or doing the name game. This is all done while the dog is on leash. (2 – 3 minutes).

2. Using a 50 ft leash with some distance between you and the dog, apply leash pressure by pulling the leash tight enough to encourage the dog to come towards you. Verbal encouragement may be given to help lure the dog towards you. This can be fun sounds like "pup pup pup," or kissy noises. Once the dog has committed to coming, release pressure. Once the dog is about 10 ft (or at the current working distance) away from you, give the recall command. Prompting the dog to sit at the end should no longer be required.

3. Once the dog is sitting in front of you, mark the behavior with a positive marker and maintain eye contact for about 2 or 3 seconds before delivering a reward. This will set the standard of not coming and immediately running away from you. (3 – 5 minutes)

4. Disengage by walking around a bit and give your dog the chance to create distance from you. If needed, enlist the help of a second person to get the dog's attention, or also have them do a recall with the same standard to create the distance. (1 – 2 minutes)

5. Repeat steps 3 and 4. Still prompting recall about 10 ft (or current working distance) while working up to 50 ft away from you. Including toys or treats on the floor that the dog must ignore. (2-3 minutes)

6. End session with a few known commands, like sit, or prompt your dog with a name or look command. (2 minutes)

Lesson: Assuming you have done prior recall training, prompting can be done further at the distance trained until 50 ft is achieved.

Part 2

Exactly like the basics, you start with the foundation of the ideal training goal. In this scenario, I want to build more distractions and get rid of the long line completely. Before getting to that step, I want to make sure my dog understands the working distance. Your dog might have a good recall at 10 ft away, but once the dog is past that, it's a new ball game. So, get your dog to a comfortable working distance, but also train at that distance. Train recalls with varied conditions, as you will learn more about in the proofing section.

Recall 400: The Advanced Recall Session

Training Goal: Recall training from 50 ft away (with low distractions)

Methods: Shaping and positive reinforcement

Training tools needed: Dog's preferred reward (treats, toys, or tugs)

Training the 'recall' command will always be done in a controlled and enclosed environment for safety. Make sure to include any distractions that might interfere with the behavior for the training goal. As your dog progresses, we will start to introduce more distractions or difficulties at a gradual pace. Once your area is prepped, training can start.

1. Start with social play to get your dog focused and engaged. This consists of having the dog chase you a bit, playing tug, or doing the name game. This is all done while the dog is off leash. (2 – 3 minutes).
2. Using a 50 ft leash with some distance between you and the dog. Give the recall command and apply leash pressure by pulling the leash tight enough to encourage the dog to come towards you. Once the dog has committed to coming, release pressure. Prompting the dog to sit at the end should no longer be required.
3. Once the dog is sitting in front of you, mark the behavior with a positive marker and maintain eye contact for about 2 or 3 seconds before delivering a reward. This will set the standard of not coming and immediately running away from you. (3 – 5 minutes)
4. Disengage by walking around a bit and give your dog the chance to create distance from you. If needed, enlist the help of a second

person to get the dog's attention, or also do a recall with the same standard to create distance. (1 – 2 minutes)

5. Repeat steps 3 and 4. Still prompting recall about 50 ft away from you. Including toys or treats on the floor that the dog must ignore. Gradually start to fade out leash pressure until it's not needed.

6. End the session with a few known commands, like sit, or prompt your dog with a name or look command. (2 minutes)

Lesson: This session should be held at a dog park with minimal dogs present or in an enclosed area with other distractions.

The recall command should be used daily. This command pairs well with other commands and manners throughout the dog's daily routine. Recalling your dog to come in/out of the house for potty breaks, walks, to get in the car, and for meals or play time. Those are just a few examples that I can think of that prove recall is a daily command. I always recommend using a leash or long line when working dogs in public to be in compliance with local law. Even if your dog has a great recall, I recommend using good judgment in all situations to ensure the safety of your canine companion.

Training "Leave it and Drop it"

I will start each command with how important the commands are because they are the primary commands after all. I remember when I was being trained as a professional dog trainer, and one of my mentors talked about the importance of 'leave it' and 'drop it.' Both commands are life-saving and work in different ways. These are typically known as the mouth commands because they pertain to how the dog chooses to use its mouth. 'Leave it,' however, I defined as more of a focus command because it means eyes off whatever you are looking at and refocus on me. 'Drop it' is, in fact, a mouth command because it speaks to the dog dropping whatever it has picked up.

Imagine you are home from surgery and recovering, but when you go to take your prescribed medicine, you drop the pill bottle, and it spills all over the floor. Your dog rushes over to sample this weird floor treat. This was the example that made me understand why 'leave it' can be lifesaving. Similarly, 'drop it' can also be used in a different scenario where your dog has picked up a diseased or poisoned animal. No one wants to play tug of war with a dead rodent. There are three methods I use to teach "leave it": two are practically the same, the Hand method and the Foot method, and the other is the leash method. Let's dive right in.

Leave it 101: The basics

Training Goal: Setting the foundation for the "leave it" command

Methods: Shaping, Positive reinforcement, and leash pressure (as needed)

Training tools needed: leash, preferred reward, secondary less preferred reward

Training the 'leave it' command will always be done in a controlled environment for safety. Make sure to minimize or eliminate any distractions that might interfere with the behavior for the training goal. As your dog progresses, we will start to introduce more distractions or difficulties at a gradual pace. Once your area is prepped, training can start.

1. Start with social play to get your dog focused and engaged. This consists of having the dog chase you a bit, playing tug, or doing the name game. This is all done while the dog is on a leash. (2 – 3 minutes).

2. Hand method: Starting in a kneeling position or sitting on the floor with your dog nearby, you will place the less preferred reward on the floor. Using your hand to cover it but keep space between your fingers so that the dog can smell the treat. Encourage the dog's attention to the treat but prevent them from accessing the treat. Make a sound that draws their attention to you, get eye contact, mark this behavior, and deliver a higher value treat. (3 – 5 minutes).

   Foot method: Starting in a standing position with your dog nearby, you will place the less preferred reward on the floor. Using your foot to cover it by using your heel as a pivot point to swivel the end of your foot over the treat. Make sure to hover above the treat and not crush it on the bottom of your shoe. Encourage your dog's attention to the treat by tapping your foot near it or pointing but prevent them from accessing the treat. Make a sound that draws their attention to you, get eye contact, mark this behavior, and deliver a higher value treat (3 – 5 minutes).

Leash Method: Starting in a standing position with your dog nearby. Toss the less preferred reward on the floor just a bit beyond the length of your leash, making sure the dog sees you toss the treat. When the dog hits the end of the leash, encourage them to come back to you with leash pressure as needed (release pressure when they start returning to you). Make eye contact when they come to you, mark this behavior, and deliver a higher-value treat. Alternatively, with this method, you can mark the moment when the dog looks at you (3-5 minutes).

3. Allow your dog to go back to the bait treat with the leash method. You might need to toss another treat if the dog doesn't automatically go back to the first treat. If using the hand or foot method, draw the dog's attention back to the bait treat. Again, make a sound that draws the dog's attention to you, get eye contact, mark the behavior, and deliver a higher-value treat. Repeat steps 2 and 3 several times (3- 5 minutes).

4. After about ten times or so, start to prompt the dog with the 'leave it' command. If the dog doesn't look immediately, repeat the sound from the previous step to get the dog's attention. Again, get eye contact, mark the behavior, and deliver a higher value treat. Repeat this process until the behavior is paired with the cue (3 – 5 minutes). Over several sessions for proficiency.

5. End the session with a known command like 'sit' or even a successful 'leave it'. At the end of the session, make sure to remove bait treats from the floor and not allow the dog to get them. This will undo the point of the training session entirely (1-2 minutes).

Part 2

🔑 *Pro tip*: Try using a "Jackpot" reward. Providing numerous treats one after another makes reinforcement more appealing for the behavior.

Part 2

Drop it 101: The Basics

Training Goal: Setting the foundation for the "Drop it" command.

Methods: Luring, capturing, and positive reinforcement

Training tools: Preferred toy and preferred treat, long line (15 ft)

Training the 'drop it' command will always be done in a controlled environment for safety. Make sure to minimize or eliminate any distractions that might interfere with the behavior for the training goal. As your dog progresses, we will start to introduce more distractions or difficulties at a gradual pace. Once your area is prepped, training can start.

1. Start with social play to get your dog focused and engaged. This consists of playing tug. This is all done while the dog is on a long line. (2 – 3 minutes).
2. Continue to engage in the game of tug. Make sure to have a treat ready in your other hand without your dog knowing. This should be done while the dog is focused on the tug toy. Stop playing tug by holding the toy still and firm. Present the treat. When the dog opens its mouth, mark with a positive marker and reward the behavior. Repeat this step several times. (3- 5 minutes). **Skip the next step if this is your behavioral goal.**
3. Just like the step above, engage in tug-of-war, then stop playing. This time, you will present the treat but allow the toy to drop to the floor/ground. Mark the behavior with a positive marker immediately when the dog drops the toy. Reward the dog. Repeat this step several times. (3-5 minutes) **Skip step 2 if this is your behavior goal.**
4. Using steps 2 or 3 as the framework, depending on whether you are training the dog to drop something in your hand or to drop it on the ground. You will repeat the preferred step this time, prompting the behavior "drop it" or "Hand" before presenting the treat. Mark the behavior with a positive marker and reward. Repeat this step several times. (3 – 5 minutes)

Part 2

5. In this step, we will eliminate the treat as the reward by doing the following steps. Prompt the behavior "drop it" or "hand." When the dog gives the appropriate response, mark the behavior with a positive marker and reward by resuming the game of tug-of-war. (3 – 5 minutes)
   *If your dog isn't into tug, choose a reward they genuinely enjoy and follow the same Drop-It sequence.
6. End the session by letting the dog win the tug of war game.

Pro tip: You can teach both commands separately. One behavior is to have the dog put an item in your hand, and another command is to drop the item. 'Hand' is a great foundation for service dog work.

Leave it 350: Advanced Leave it Training

Training Goal: Teaching "leave it" off-leash

Methods: Positive and Negative reinforcement, Leash Pressure, Shaping

Training tools needed: Preferred Treat, Decoy reward, 15 ft long line

Training the 'leave it' command will always be done in a controlled environment for safety. Make sure to include any distractions that might interfere with the behavior for the training goal. As your dog progresses, we will gradually introduce more distractions or challenges. Once your area is prepped, training can start. The decoy reward should be placed along a linear path about 3 - 4 ft apart from each other. This should be done in several sessions, adjusting placement until the dog can walk right over the decoys without showing interest. Toys and treats can be placed on the ground when the dog progresses to this level of training. Decoy rewards can be homemade plastic containers with holes to prevent the dog from getting the treats inside.

1. Start with social play to get your dog focused and engaged. This consists of playing tug. This is all done while the dog is on a long line. (2 – 3 minutes).
2. Place three or four decoys (treats inside a homemade container with holes small enough to keep the reward inside) along a path

Part 2

on the floor. With the dog on leash, walk past the decoys at a distance where the dog shows interest but not close enough for them to touch the decoy. When the dog looks at the decoy, prompt with "leave it." When the dog gives the appropriate response, mark the behavior with a positive marker and reward. Gradually get closer to the decoys (3 – 5 minutes).

3. Repeat step two over several sessions until the success rate is high, and the dog is ready to progress to step four. (1 – 2 minutes)

4. Place "free" treats (treats not in a container) on the ground in a linear path that you will walk the dog passed. Starting with the treats at a distance where the dog shows interest but still complies with the prompt. Mark and reward appropriate behavior. Move closer to treats gradually. Be patient, this could take several sessions before reducing the distance.

5. End the session on a foundational command like 'sit.' Make sure to remove any decoys or treats from the ground and never let the dog pick them up after you have prompted the dog to 'leave it.' (2 minutes)

Pro tip: Once your dog hits about a **90% success rate** with *leave it*, switch to a **long line**. Then slowly **add distance** and **reduce reliance on the line** until you can fade it out completely.

Drop it 350: Drop it Advanced Training

Training Goal: Drop it command with distance (Not applicable for 'Hand' command)

Methods: Shaping and positive reinforcement

Training tools needed: Dog's preferred toy and preferred treat

Training the 'drop it' command will always be done in a controlled environment for safety. Make sure to include any distractions that might interfere with the behavior for the training goal. As your dog progresses, we will gradually introduce more distractions or challenges. Once your area is prepped, training can start.

Part 2

1. Start with social play to get your dog focused and engaged. This consists of playing tug. This is all done while the dog is on a long line. (2 – 3 minutes).

2. Continue to engage in the game of tug. Stop playing tug by letting go of the toy. Prompt the behavior with the "Drop it" command. Mark immediately for an appropriate response and reward. Repeat the step several times. The frequency of reward should vary by requiring a different number of correct responses. The first three times, the dog gets a reward. Then the dog needs to do 3 successful 'drop it' for a reward. The reward system should vary often, like a slot machine. (3- 5 minutes). **Skip the next step if this is your behavioral goal.**

3. Just like the step above, engage in tug-of-war, then stop playing by letting go of the toy. This time, you will present your open hand to your dog. Prompt the behavior with the "Hand" command. Mark immediately for an appropriate response and reward. Repeat the step several times. The reward system should vary often. (3-5 minutes) **Skip step two if this is your behavior goal.**

4. Using steps 2 or 3 as the framework, depending on whether you are training the dog to drop something in your hand or to drop it on the ground. You will repeat the preferred step this time for additional practice (3-5 minutes).

5. In this step, we will gradually add distance. This is only applicable to the dropping item on the ground. With the dog on a long line, engage in tug of war. Allow the dog to win and create space, only about a foot or so. Prompt the 'drop it' command (encouragement might be needed with a treat). Mark immediately for an appropriate response and reward by resuming the tug game or by recalling and giving a treat. Repeat the step several times over many sessions, increasing the distance to the preferred training goal. (3 – 5 minutes)

6. End the session by letting the dog win the tug of war game (3 – 5 minutes).

Part 2

Training Stay/wait

These are core commands that all beginning obedience classes will cover. This is great when helping your dog work through impulse control. This command can make the difference between your dog running after a squirrel and staying by your side. This could be the command that keeps your dog from jumping on a person at a pet store. So, this is where the dog's behavior is the same for two different commands, but it's how they end that makes the difference. Stay is a permanent hold, and wait is more of a temporary hold. I want you to think of 'stay' as I will be right back. Whereas wait is more of let me go ahead, and I will meet you there. What that means is when you release your dog from a 'stay', you **must** return to the dog. Compared to 'wait,' you can release your dog at any distance; this is great to pair with recall.

The steps and methods for both behaviors are the same. Some pro tips for training sessions: do only one of these behaviors in a single training session. Don't alternate between them to reduce confusion. Always mark the end of the behavior by using the "release" command. This is one of the commands that can have an ambiguous ending. Your dog knows that a sit has come to an end when their butt hits the ground. So it is crucial to always 'release' your dog from a hold command.

Stay and wait 101: The basics of holding positions

Training Goal: Introduction to hold commands, stay/wait (with low distractions)

Methods: Positive reinforcement, Capturing

Training tools needed: Dog's preferred reward, leash (or long line), and cot/bed (optional)

Training the 'stay/wait' command will always be done in a controlled and enclosed environment for safety. Make sure to minimize and eliminate any distractions that might interfere with the behavior for the training goal. As your dog progresses, we will start to introduce more distractions or difficulties at a gradual pace. Once your area is prepped, training can start.

Part 2

1. Start with social play to get your dog focused and engaged. This consists of having the dog chase you a bit, playing tug, or doing the name game. This is all done while the dog is on a leash or long line. (2 – 3 minutes).
2. Prompt your dog to sit. Mark behavior with a yes and maintain eye contact. If needed, hold a treat where the dog can see it but not reach it. The goal is to keep the dog holding the 'sit.' Mark again and deliver the treat. Encourage the dog to get up and repeat. Gradually increasing how long the dog holds the 'sit.' (3 – 5 minutes)
3. Prompt the dog to sit. This time, try moving one foot back from the dog while holding your hand out in a stop gesture. Don't move too fast and encourage the dog to maintain the 'sit' by maintaining eye contact. Repeat this step, trying to get one full step away from the dog. Release the dog from the hold. You might need to encourage the dog to get up (1 – 2 minutes).
4. Move around a bit while the dog follows you. Prompt the dog to sit. This time, pair the command 'stay' with the hand gesture. The requirement should only be about 3 to 5 seconds at this point. Mark the behavior with a good this time, not a 'yes,' then 'release and give a treat. Repeat this step with the verbal and hand gesture over several sessions, trying to build up the time and the amount of distance you can get from your dog. (3 – 5 minutes)
5. End the session with a known command, like sit, or use your dog's name to get its attention. (2 minutes)

Stay and wait 301: The advanced holding positions

Training Goal: Advance hold commands, stay/wait (with distractions and distance)

Methods: Positive reinforcement, Capturing

Training tools needed: Dog's preferred reward, leash (or long line), and cot/bed (optional)

Part 2

Training the 'stay/wait' command will always be done in a controlled and enclosed environment for safety. Make sure to include any distractions that might interfere with the behavior for the training goal. As your dog progresses, we will start to introduce more distractions or difficulties at a gradual pace. Once your area is prepped, training can start.

1. Start with social play, to get your dog focused and engaged. This consists of having the dog chase you a bit, playing tug, or doing the name game. This is all done while the dog is on a leash or long line. (2 – 3 minutes).

2. Prompt your dog to sit and stay. Mark behavior with a 'good' and maintain eye contact. The goal is to keep the dog holding the 'sit.' Mark again with good and take 1 – 2 steps back from the dog. If the dog holds the sit-stay, mark with a 'yes' and return to deliver a treat, encouraging the dog to stay. Then, release the dog and enable it to get up and repeat. Gradually increasing how long the dog holds the 'sit' and the number of steps you take (3 – 5 minutes)

    Pro tip: Holds are the exception to the saying it once rule. You can repeat the hold command periodically to remind your dog that they are still on a hold.

3. Prompt your dog to sit-stay. Marking with a 'good' when you get the appropriate response this time taking more steps away and returning to the dog. Repeat the hold command and step away again. Repeat this for several trials, ending by returning to the dog. Marking with a "good stay" and delivering a reward. Release the dog and repeat. This should be repeated over several steps with the goal of slowly and gradually increasing distance and duration. The goal should be to introduce more distractions (2 – 5 minutes).

4. End the session with a known command, like sit, or use your dog's name to get its attention. (2 minutes)

Part 2

Training Loose Leash Walking

The most unnatural thing we train our dogs to do is walk on a leash. Some might even say it's one of the hardest commands because there are so many layers to it. We have reactivity, leash aggression, and pulling, among other issues. I will give some tips about leash walking before we get into the steps. This command could have a small book or a full chapter alone because of all the methods and techniques used for this behavior.

Some noteworthy things that I want to highlight as important aspects of loose leash walking. When walking, it's very natural to say "*come on.*" However, if we are using 'come' as the recall command, that can be confusing. When walking, use 'let's go' as a verbal command to get your dog to walk with you. As the name applies, loose leash walking means there should be slack in the leash. When the leash is taut or there is tension, we want to communicate a correction or dislike in behavior. If the walk always has pressure on the leash, that becomes communication; keep moving instead of correcting. When walking, the leash should never be tight for more than a second unless correcting. What side does your dog walk on? This should be the same every time and with every person in the house. This prevents your dog from crossing in front of you and potentially tripping you. Some people like to walk their dog to the left and will travel to where the dog is on the inside and away from traffic. This is a personal preference, but whatever side you pick, stick with it.

There are tons of walking devices, harnesses, and tools. I want you guys to understand that a collar is used for identification only. In emergencies, yes, attach the leash to the collar, but when training, a flat collar should never be used for walking. This can get controversial as far as what to use, so I won't go into details about it. I will say that no matter what tool you decide to use, make sure to consult a trainer or do research about the proper placement or fit, and technique for that specific walking tool. There are head halters, slip leads, front clipping harnesses, back clipping harnesses, prong collars, choke chains, etc. I think in the right hands, any of these can be used effectively. However, in uneducated hands, they can all be used wrong. The technique I will be outlining assumes that you are using proper techniques with any of those tools. This highlights the steps of walking and not using any specific tool. So, adjust as needed for your specific walking device. However, it's universal that leash pressure is a form of communication when applying appropriate amounts of pressure to the leash and walking device. The dog turns the pressure off by complying or behaving appropriately. Leash pressure should never be used in an abusive manner.

There are specific methods for introducing a leash to puppies and dogs with little to no experience with a leash. The first step is making a positive association with the leash without any pressure. This can be done by showing the leash and providing rewards for the dog showing mild interest. This will progress to attaching the leash to the dog and rewarding. Next, allow the dog to drag the leash around a safe area in short intervals over several days. These steps should be followed with any walking device. You want to desensitize the dog to the tools.

Loose leash walking 101: The basics

Training Goal: Introduction to leash communication

Methods: Luring, shaping, and positive reinforcement

Training tools needed: 6ft leash and dog's preferred reward (treats, toys, or tugs)

Training loose leash walking should start in an environment with no distractions, which can be done in the backyard. Training walks are broken into three phases: social play, training, and leisure time. When teaching a dog leash manners, it's important to focus on the quality of the behavior instead of quantity (length of walk). Training walks should be done twice a day, starting with a bit of exercise or playing in the backyard before the walk to taper some of the dog's excess energy. I prefer to walk my dog before feeding, so they are still motivated for the treats I provide.

Phase 1: Social play and engagement

1. Start with social play to get your dog focused and engaged. This consists of having the dog chase you a bit, playing tug, or doing

the name game. This is all done while the dog is on leash. (2 – 3 minutes).

Phase 2: Training

2. Using a 6 ft leash, start with your dog in a sit on the side that is designated for walking, facing the same direction. Prompt the dog's name while giving the 'let's go' command and moving forward. The dog should remain on the side of you from their shoulder to the middle of their body. Take a few steps while luring with a treat and giving praise while the dog is using the correct pace. Rewards can be given while in motion, as we want to reward good walking. When you stop walking, prompt your dog to sit. Mark behavior and then reward. Repeat this several times, varying the number of steps you take. (3-5 minutes)

3. Starting the same way as in step 2, you can also do different walking patterns like figure 8, ovals, squares, change speed from slow to fast, and fast to slow. Variety will encourage your dog to pay attention to your movements. Use treats to lure your dog through left turns and right turns or to follow you at the correct pace. Slowly start to remove the lure and progress to giving rewards for the correct pace. For example, provide a reward for every odd number: 1, 3, 5, and 7 steps. Then provide a reward for every 3 steps, then every 5 steps, and then at every stop. (3- 5 minutes)

Pro tip: Correction and redirection will be frequent at the beginning of training. Be patient and review loose leash drills and troubleshooting in the 'Worksheets and Training Tools' section at the end of this book.

Phase 3: Leisure phase.

4. This phase is very easy. This is where you allow the dog to sniff around and have a bit of dog time on the leash. This should be treated as a reward for all the work they did during training. (1 – 2 minutes)

5. Repeat steps 1 through 4 over several sessions, increasing the level of distractions as your dog progresses. Make sure to remain

Part 2

within the threshold of the dog as you progress to more difficulty and reduce the threshold properly.

6. End the session with a known command, like sit, or prompting your dog with a name or look command. (2 minutes)

Pro tip: Repeat training over several weeks with consistency and gradually increasing difficulty.

Loose leash walking 301: Advanced loose leash walking

Training Goal: Leash walking with distractions and commands

Methods: Luring, shaping, and positive reinforcement

Training tools needed: 6ft leash and dog's preferred reward (treats, toys, or tugs)

Training loose leash walking should have now graduated to an environment with added distractions, which can be done in areas like the neighborhood, pet-friendly stores, and parks. Training walks are broken into three phases: social play, training, and leisure time. When teaching a dog leash manners, it's important to focus on the quality of the behavior instead of quantity (length of walk). Training walks should be done twice a day, starting with a bit of exercise or playing in the backyard before the walk to taper some of the dog's excess energy. I prefer to walk my dog before feeding, so they are still motivated for the treats I provide.

Phase 1: Social play and engagement

1. Start with social play to get your dog focused and engaged. This consists of having the dog chase you a bit, playing tug, or doing the name game. This is all done while the dog is on leash. (2 – 3 minutes).

Phase 2: Training

2. Using a 6 ft leash, start with your dog in a sit on the side that is designated for walking, facing the same direction. Prompt the dog's name while giving the 'let's go' command and moving forward. The dog should remain on the side of you from their

shoulder to the middle of their body. Take any number of steps without luring with a treat. You should be able to gain focus with the dog's name and provide a reward for the correct pace. Rewards can be given while in motion, as we want to reward good walking. When you stop walking, the dog should sit automatically. Mark the behavior and then reward. Repeat this several times, varying the number of steps you take. (3-5 minutes)

💡 Pro tips: Correction and redirection should become more infrequent at this level of training. Review loose leash drills and troubleshooting in the *"Worksheets and Training Tools"* section at the end of this book.

Phase 3: Leisure phase.

3. This phase is very easy. This is where you allow the dog to sniff around and have a bit of dog time on the leash. This should be treated as a reward for all the work they did during training. (1 – 2 minutes)
4. Repeat steps 1 through 3 over several sessions, increasing the level of distractions as your dog progresses. Make sure to remain within the threshold of the dog as you progress to more difficulty, and reduce the threshold properly.
5. End the session with a known command, like sit, or prompting your dog with a name or look command. (2 minutes)

Training Stop (drop)

This command is probably the most advanced on the list. This is assuming you have done solid recall training, and the dog knows the "down" command with distance. This command combines several of the foundational commands into one. The Stop/drop command is used when your dog is about to run across a busy street. The dog will drop into a down position and stay. This could be used if your dog charges over to say hello to the neighbor who doesn't like dogs. I will mention again that this command requires some prerequisites. The dog knows: recall with distance and distractions, down from a stand with distractions, has a good,

Part 2

solid hold, and has impulse control. Once you have had high success in those commands, you can move on to this command, which will take time.

Drop (Stop) 401: The basics

Training Goal: Drop Foundation (with no distractions)

Methods: Shaping, luring, and positive reinforcement

Training tools needed: Dog's preferred reward (treats, toys, or tugs) and a long line

Training the 'drop' command will always be done in a controlled and enclosed environment for safety. Make sure to minimize or eliminate any distractions that might interfere with the behavior for the training goal. As your dog progresses, we will start to introduce more distractions and gradually increase difficulties. Once your area is prepped, training can start.

1. Start with social play to get your dog focused and engaged. This should be done with the dog on a leash or long line. (2 – 3 minutes).
2. Introduce down while moving will be done in phases. First, you will just get the dog 'down' from a standing position. Repeat this first phase several times. Prompt, mark the behavior, and reward. Next, you will add distance between yourself and the dog, starting at 2 or 3 feet away and gradually working up to your training goal. I typically try to get up to 20 feet away from my dog. Repeat this second phase several times. Prompt, mark the behavior, and reward (5 – 7 minutes).
3. Introducing the drop while moving, this step will have the dog walking next to you. Take several steps forward before quickly prompting the dog to 'drop.' If needed, lure down with a reward. If the dog seems confused because it doesn't know the drop command, pair it with the down command right after (3-5 minutes).
4. Once the dog has associated the new cue with the associated behavior of down, you can remove the down cue. Repeat this

Part 2

several times. Walk prompt, mark the behavior, and reward. During this phase, it's a good idea to introduce a faster pace (3 – 5 minutes).

5. Next, you will have the dog walking towards you while walking backwards. At the start, you will only walk back and stop to prompt the dog to drop. After the dog understands, you will start to step forward to block the dog's path to get an immediate drop. Repeat this phase several times. Prompt, mark behavior, and reward (3 – 5 minutes).

6. Over several sessions, you will repeat steps 1 through 5. You can introduce a barrier for the dog not to cross, like a broomstick or PVC pipe. You start with the barrier dividing you from the dog and prompt a down several times. You can throw a treat behind the dog to help create space, and when they come back to the barrier, have them down again. I don't particularly like this method because I don't want the dog to become dependent on the barrier. However, if properly used and faded out, it can be a great method (3 – 5 minutes).

7. Repeat steps 3- 5 several times. Now building up to the dog being 5-10 ft away, prompting the recall, followed by the drop. You might need to step forward into the dog's path to get it to understand what is being asked. Repeat this several times over several sessions. (3 – 5 minutes)

8. End the session with a known command, like sit, or prompting your dog with their name or look command. (2 minutes)

Drop (Stop) 410: The advanced drop command

Training Goal: Drop advanced training from a distance (with distractions)

Methods: Shaping, luring, and positive reinforcement

Training tools needed: Dog's preferred reward (treats, toys, or tugs)

Training the 'drop' command will always be done in a controlled and enclosed environment for safety. Make sure to include any distractions

Part 2

that might interfere with the behavior for the training goal. As your dog progresses, we will start to introduce more distractions and gradually increase difficulties. Once your area is prepped, training can start.

1. Start with social play to get your dog focused and engaged. This should be done with the dog off-leash. (2 – 3 minutes).

2. In this stage, the dog has graduated from the basics to this level of training. The dog understands the drop command now, so we will slowly add more distance and distractions. First, get a baseline by completing a few successful trials of drop at the current working distance with no distraction. Repeat several times. Next, add a distraction of a person or another known dog at a safe distance. Prompt the drop, mark behavior, and reward. Repeat this step several times before moving to the next step. (3 – 5 minutes

3. Now, remove the distraction and increase the distance. Train at this distance for several trials before reintroduction of the distraction. Prompt, mark behavior, and reward. Bring distraction back into the training area and repeat several times. (3 – 5 minutes)

4. Repeat steps 2 and 3, gradually increasing distance and distractions. Slowly train to move the distractions closer to the recall path of the dog. If the dog fails. Reset with the distraction a bit further from the failed trial distance. Repeat several times over several sessions (3 – 5 minutes)

5. Repeat steps 3 and 4 several times. Building up to the training goal that you have set. Introduce distractions like sounds, throwing balls, toys, and other dogs (this one will be extremely hard). Repeat this several times over several sessions. (3 – 5 minutes)

6. End the session with a known command, like sit, or prompt your dog with a name or look command. (2 minutes)

Part 2

Review:

This concludes the training section of the book. I provided a general structure and outline that can be used for any behavior, with some methods that can be used with any training philosophy that works for you. I hope that you find value in this section and use this book as a guide on your training journey. I encourage you all to read many books and guides to get a comprehensive view of dog training from others in the industry. I wanted to give some reminders before moving into the next part of the book. Remember, training is a bonding experience with your dog that will have its ups and downs. No two training sessions are the same, and once you think you've mastered something, you take a few steps back. Try not to be discouraged by setbacks, but learn and adapt. There was a lot of information in this section. I summarized the major takeaways below.

Key Takeaways

- **Rules for Dog Training**
    1. Never lie to your dog – Don't change the rules when you set them, be consistent
    2. The Rule of **ONE** – One command per behavior, say commands once, and one second to reinforce behavior
    3. Never get frustrated. Control yourself to control your dog
    4. Consistency is key, trust the process, keep training.
- **Training Session Structure**
1. Keep training sessions short, 15 – 20 minutes max.
2. Start all training with some form of social play or engagement
3. Keep training fun and engaging; the more fun, the more they learn
4. The number of behaviors taught in a single session should be 2 max.

- **Training essentials**
    1. Leash – lightweight and durable 6 ft lead.
    2. Rewards – this can vary from food, toys, or attention.
    3. Longline- lightweight and durable 15 ft, 20 ft, or 30 ft line.
    4. Treat Pouch – Something that has separate pockets to divide different values of treats recommended.

5. Cot/bed – A Lightweight, portable cot or mat that can be transported with you from location to location.
- **Training Methods**
    1. Luring – This method uses a toy or treat to guide your dog into a desired behavior.
    2. Shaping – This method is used to teach complex behaviors by rewarding smaller behaviors that progress to the overall behavior.
    3. Capturing – This method is waiting for your dog to do some desired behavior naturally.

I can't say it enough, but make sure to consistently train and train. The more consistent the better the results, when using proper training techniques and methods. Don't be afraid to make small mistakes; use them as opportunities to learn.

Part 3: Time to Proof

(Train, Test, Repeat)

What exactly is Proofing?

Proofing is probably my favorite aspect of dog training because it encapsulates everything dog training is truly about. It's a process of testing desired behaviors in a variety of environments to ensure reliability, no matter the distraction or situation. I like to think of it as the quality assurance department of dog training. This is where all the pieces come together, setting a standard for what a trained dog should consistently be able to do in every situation. Proofing is what separates a dog that's trained from a truly well-trained dog. To help drive the point home, I'll walk you through two scenarios centered around the command 'stay,' which is one of the top three lifesaving commands and a cornerstone of my primary commands list.

In scenario one, we meet Rufus, a dog with a solid *stay* command in the backyard. His owner hasn't taken him out in public much but tries to stay consistent with training at home and daily walks. After about eight months of working with Rufus, the owner gets invited to a picnic. Friends encourage him to bring Rufus along, praising how well-behaved he seems. At the picnic, Rufus is doing great on a 25-foot-long line. The owner is proud of his progress; people are asking about training tips and admiring how well Rufus is doing. Someone asks to see a trick, so the owner decides to show off Rufus's *stay*. He removes the long line, places Rufus in a sit-stay, and walks 15 feet away. This is the same distance they practiced at home. Everything *seems* perfect… until, just before being released, Rufus breaks the stay and bolts. Thankfully, in this scenario, Rufus is okay. No one gets hurt. But it's a wake-up call.

Now, let's look at scenario two. Fido, unlike Rufus, gets regular real-world training. His owner slowly and intentionally exposes him to new environments, distractions, and stimuli. He doesn't assume Fido knows a command until he's shown an 80% or higher success rate across different conditions. So, when Fido goes to a picnic, he behaves just as well as he does at home. The only reason he's put in a *stay* at all is because the owner steps away to help someone and doesn't have time to grab the leash. Fido holds his stay because he's trained for this exact type of unpredictability. Now, let's compare. First, dog training shouldn't be about impressing your friends. It's an essential responsibility for keeping your dog—and everyone around them—safe in the human world we've brought them into. Dogs should always be on a leash or long line unless they're actively working or competing in a controlled environment. That said, we're human. I've even walked my dog to the mailbox off-leash. I left Rufus's story open-ended on purpose. Any number of things could have caused him to break the stay: a squirrel, a loud sound, excitement, or fear. That's the point. Without proper proofing, we roll the dice. Now, to be clear: I'm anti-leash and pro-training. What I mean is, a leash should be a *backup*, not a steering wheel. If your dog is only manageable because of the leash, you're not really in control. Real control comes from proofed obedience.

How does all of this connect to proofing?

As we saw in the earlier examples, reliable obedience isn't just about knowing a command; it's about being able to perform it anywhere, anytime, under any condition. Life is unpredictable, and that's where proofing becomes essential. Proofing is a process that combines behavioral psychology, learning theory, and operant conditioning. The core pillars for proofing are generalization, consistency, and real-world reliability.

Dogs often become overwhelmed when faced with multiple distractions at once. This can result in cognitive overload, which can cause your dog's focus to decrease and lead to unwanted behaviors. The goal is to make stimuli as neutral as possible, meaning your dog doesn't have an emotional reaction to the dog walking by or the stranger you encounter on your morning walk. If we can pair calm, neutral behaviors or positive associations with stimuli, we can get the dog to generalize behaviors in a variety of environments and encounters.

This contrasts with the idea of discriminating behaviors to only specific environments, like your home, for example. Proofing connects doing any behavior in any location, with any distraction, no matter the distance. Through repeated exposure to different distractions, the more generalized those distractions become. However, it's not just exposing the dog to distractions. It's training your dog and pairing positive experiences with the distraction that makes the difference.

Proofing, in this regard, uses principles of Pavlov's classical conditioning to achieve desensitization and lessen the emotional response to distractions. In terms of learning theory, proofing employs operant conditioning. When the dog exhibits the desired behavior and follows a command, it is rewarded: positive reinforcement. Conversely, when the dog fails to comply or breaks the desired behavior, the reward is withheld, which is negative punishment. This allows the dog to control the outcome by choosing to perform the desired behavior to earn a reward, regardless of environmental distractions. This principle is based on the work of Skinner.

Another aspect is varying the reward schedule to strengthen the behavioral response through the unpredictability of rewards, similar to a slot machine schedule. Humans keep pulling the lever because at some point, they will get a reward, and the size of the reward often doesn't even matter. This unpredictability also strengthens the motivation to continue the behavior.

That's a brief summary of the science behind proofing. It's a combination of many different aspects of behavior and learning theory to ensure reliability. There are many books and articles written on those topics that I encourage you all to research further. Understanding proofing as a method of cementing behaviors is using decades of scientific research, without even knowing it. So, thank the scholars who built the foundation and those who connected the dots, providing the framework that allows our dogs to learn and achieve incredible feats.

Next, I'll walk you through the six requirements of proofing and how I apply them to every command using what I call *the proofing wheel*.

First, let's go over each of the proofing requirements and define what they mean. That way, as we move forward, you'll be able to clearly follow along when I refer to one part of the process versus another. The order I present them in reflects how I typically move through the *proofing wheel*, but depending on your dog, training goals, or personal style, you might

Part 3

start at a different point—and that's perfectly fine, as long as you're using the same criteria.

You've probably heard of the "Three Ds" of dog training: **distraction, distance**, and **duration**. These form the foundation of all proofing work. Through my own research and real-world experience, I've expanded on these principles and created a more comprehensive framework I call *the proofing wheel*. This includes three additional criteria: **latency, precision,** and **speed**.

These aren't new ideas, but rather classic concepts reframed into a modern and intentional philosophy of training. By combining the original Three Ds with clear minimum standards for how each behavior should be performed, we create a reliable system for producing dogs that are not just trained but *well-trained*.

Each requirement comes with its own level of difficulty and builds on the last. Some stages may even be limited by external factors like environment or training tools, but they all serve the same purpose: to challenge the dog in a structured, measurable way and ensure true reliability.

1. **Distraction** – This term is self-explanatory: it's any external stimulus that competes for your dog's attention, regardless of intention. This isn't limited to just other people or animals; it could also include sounds, textures, or inanimate objects. I also like to consider your dog's emotional and mental state as a distraction if it affects their willingness to comply.

2. **Distance** – This one can be a bit tricky, as it applies differently to certain commands. Distance refers to the space between you and your dog when giving a command, as well as whether the dog still complies. This shouldn't be confused with the previously mentioned concept of *threshold*, which is different. For example, will your dog sit when you're 3 feet away? What about 12 feet? And with recall, will your dog come when you call from 10 feet away? What about 50 feet and out of sight?

Part 3

3. **Latency** – Here, we deviate slightly from the core three Ds with this concept. Latency is the time between when the command is given and when the dog begins the behavior. The response time should be short. The shorter the latency, the better.

4. **Duration** – Returning to the last of the core three D's, duration is the length of time your dog maintains a behavior. For example, does your dog pop up from a 'sit' right after being praised? This is an important element.

5. **Precision** – This refers to how the behavior should look. For instance, with a "sit" command, there's a specific posture the dog should maintain. If the dog is leaning on its hip, that's not the most precise form of a "*sit*." Precision helps define the standard you're aiming for with each behavior.

6. **Speed** – This is also a time-based measure but differs from both duration and latency. Speed refers to how quickly the dog completes the behavior once it starts. When you recall your dog, do they make a beeline toward you—or do they slowly mosey over with no sense of urgency?

Now that we've defined the requirements, we can discuss the framework for working through the **Proofing Wheel** (see Fig. 1 below). This method should only be applied to commands the dog already knows—meaning you're past the learning phase described earlier in Part 2 of this book.

I'll walk you through the framework using the *"sit"* command as an example, but keep in mind that this process applies to any behavior, with some minor adjustments depending on the command. For instance, if you're proofing a recall, always start in a fenced or enclosed area. As you progress, you can move into open areas—but always with a long line attached for safety, even if you're not actively holding it.

You might begin with a 6-foot leash, graduate to a 25-foot line, and ultimately work up to a 100-foot line. While the structure of the Proofing

Part 3

Wheel stays the same, the tools and their use may vary depending on the behavior you're working on.

Now that we understand the structure of the Proofing Wheel and how it applies to already-learned behaviors, let's walk through a practical example. I'll start with the "sit" command to demonstrate how each requirement is addressed and built upon the next.

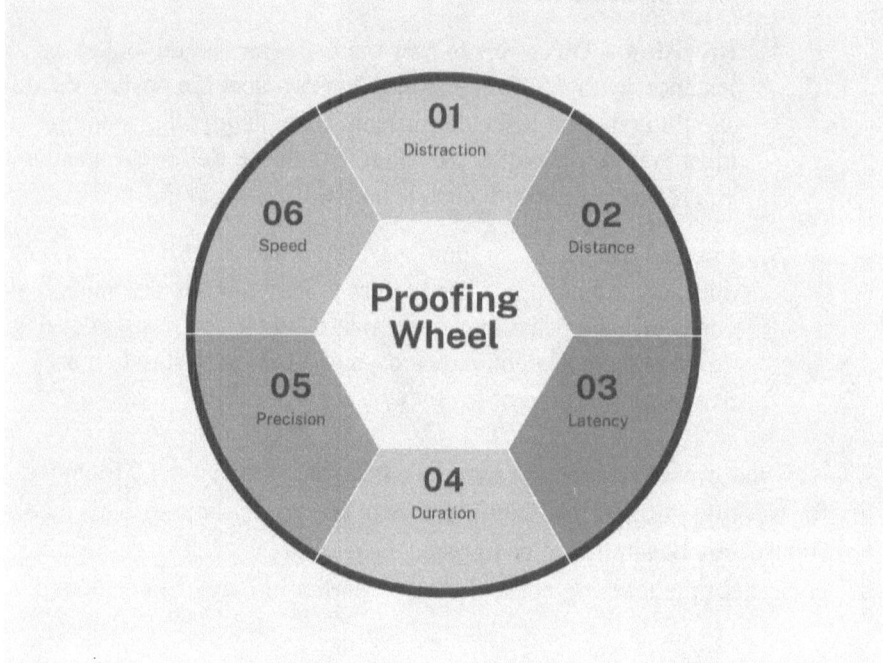

Fig. 1

Proofing and Repetition

Proofing behavior is a slow, deliberate process. It should be done with intention—none of the following steps should be skipped if you want to ensure success. To begin, the prerequisite is that the dog already knows the command and is well past the learning phase. For example, my dog can reliably perform a "sit" using either a verbal or hand signal in a no-

Part 3

distraction environment. I won't be covering how to teach or prompt the command here—if you're still working on those basics, you're not quite ready to start proofing. Instead, I'll begin with **distraction** and work my way through the **Proofing Wheel**, showing how to apply each requirement to an already-learned behavior. Keep in mind, proofing can and should be done multiple times, with different goals, even using the same command. Now, let's begin.

Step 1: Setting the Goal and Identifying Challenges

As mentioned earlier, intentionality is key in the proofing process. Establishing measurable criteria allows you to assess progress effectively. In this example, the goal is to have my dog sit politely in crowded areas, enabling visits to public, dog-friendly places without causing disturbances.

Upon assessing my dog, I identified the following triggers and responses:

- **Triggers**: Dogs, people, and shopping carts.
- **Responses**: Hypervigilance, barking, loss of focus, lunging, and jumping up.

The overall threshold distance is 25 feet from any trigger, with specific thresholds as follows:

- **Dogs**: 15 feet
- **People**: 10 feet
- **Shopping carts**: 10 feet

In terms of distraction levels (from least to most challenging):

1. Stationary shopping carts
2. People
3. Dogs (especially reactive ones)

Part 3

*All training sessions are 15 to 20 minutes long, not to overwhelm the dog. Some of the steps listed are given in an ideal training session. However, sessions will vary in many cases, very small progress is made. It's important to stay consistent and move through the process slowly and deliberately.

Step 2: Exposure and Repetition (Distraction)

Beginning with the least distracting stimulus, I employ counterconditioning and training to gradually decrease the threshold distance to the desired proximity. Starting with a stationary shopping cart, the aim is to reduce the threshold to less than 1 foot.

Initiated at a 10-foot distance from the shopping cart, I conduct a series of "sit" drills, providing positive reinforcement. The objective is to engage the dog's focus while gradually decreasing the distance to the stimulus. I reduce the distance by 2-foot increments. If the dog exhibits a negative response, I increase the distance by 3 feet from the point of reaction to regain focus. For example, moving from 10 feet to 8 feet may trigger a reaction. In that case, I step back to 11 feet. Once focus is restored, I move 2 feet closer, positioning the dog at 9 feet from the cart. If there's no negative response, I end the session there, marking that as the new threshold. Let's say the dog doesn't react negatively at 8 feet—then I would move 2 feet closer, placing me at 6 feet. If a reaction happens at that point, I step back 3 feet to 9 feet, regain focus, and then move 2 feet closer again, now at 7 feet. This process will vary depending on the stimulus and the individual dog. However, I've found this method to be the most effective. Even if the dog is doing well, I never decrease the threshold by more than 2 or 3 feet in a single session.

This process is repeated, with the distance continually decreasing in 2-foot increments. If the dog shows any negative responses, step back 3 feet to regain focus before proceeding. Reaching the desired threshold may take multiple sessions over several weeks. It's essential to let the dog set the pace to avoid overwhelming them or causing regression. Additionally, it's

Part 3

important to work with the dog at each new threshold between decreasing sessions to ensure they generalize and solidify their comfort at the new distance.

This framework applies to other triggers, such as people and dogs. When working with these triggers, I always maintain a safe distance. If I don't know the person or dog, I make sure to stay at least three feet away. I work with active participants and dogs I know well, and I always have someone on hand to ensure safety. Additionally, when using advanced training methods, it's crucial to consult with a professional dog trainer.

This step is repeated at the appropriate threshold as the distraction increases. So, for example, if the cart is moving, I will prompt the dog to sit while the cart is moving slowly and decrease the distance with the above method. As I get to the desired distance in this example, the goal would be to have the dog sit while pushing the shopping cart past us. Once I have achieved my goal, I will change the location of the stimuli and recondition as needed. Once I have exhausted all the requirements, I will reassess before moving on to the next location.

Bonus Step: Reassess and Test

This step is intended to ensure that I'm not moving the dog along the proof wheel before it's ready. I will reassess the threshold and reaction to stimuli based on the goal in various locations. I will rate this fluency out of 10 trials, looking for a success rate of 80% in all requirements.

Step 3: Increasing Distance

During this step, I will start to increase the distance from the dog to get the desired behavior. This can be a bit challenging as the dog might feel uncomfortable as you get farther away. This adds new factors that can also be a distraction: the distance between you and the dog and the emotional and mental state of the dog. I will be providing a method called "half dome" that I will provide in the reference section of this book. That

Part 3

method is a more comprehensive drill that I use when teaching a solid
'stay' or 'wait' command. That's a great drill to use at this phase of the
proofing stage with your dog.

First, we start in a no-distraction area to establish a standard for sitting at a
distance. In this example, my goal would be 10ft away from the dog to get
compliance with a 'sit' prompt. I would start by having the dog sit right in
front of me numerous times. Then I would take one step back with only
one foot and prompt the 'sit'. Once I achieve success, I will take a full
step back and prompt the dog. I will work this drill at one foot away from
the dog, looking to achieve 80% or better fluency before taking an
additional step back. Now at 2 ft, I will do a few prompts several more
times before ending the session. During my next session, I will start with
the dog right in front of me and move back to 2ft immediately to work
myself to 3ft away from the dog. I will repeat this process until I get to the
desired 10 feet away from the dog.

Once achieved in a no-distraction environment, I will start to slowly
introduce low distraction and do the same drill in various locations before
increasing the distraction. As I achieve an 80% success rate, I graduate to
new locations until I have exhausted all possible locations that my dog
and I might be. After I move to higher distraction levels, I repeat the same
process of varying the location before increasing the distraction.

Before proceeding with the following requirement, I will repeat the bonus
step: reassess and test.

Step 4: Race to the Start (Latency)

During this step of the proofing phase, I want to decrease the time from
when the command is given to when the dog starts the behavior. There is
no golden standard for how long it should take for your dog to start the
behavior. However, my personal goal is about 2 seconds or less. The way
to teach urgency is by making the reward timely and the command fun
and engaging. I achieve this by getting my dog excited through social

play. Once my dog is in high drive, I prompt my 'sit', making sure to be ready to reward within a split second. I tend to use higher value treats for immediate responses, to encourage quicker responses. The better the response, the better the reward. The most critical aspect of latency is timing and the sequence of marker to rewards. The traditional order is prompt, positive marker, and treat. The reward should never be given at the same time as the marker. In the training section, I discussed the importance and use of marker words. Using 'sit' as an example, I start my session with my dog in play. Typically, I will use tug of war or fetch to get them into the drive state. Once they are alert and focused, I will prompt with urgency. The moment my dog's butt hits the ground I reinforce and reward. During a session with 'sit,' I will get the dog to move and make an abrupt stop to sit and reinforce and reward with the same immediacy. Typically, I will only give verbal praise for any response outside of my latency window. This employs the same principles of operant conditioning that we discussed in the earlier section. As my dog starts to give the *"sit"* in the appropriate timeframe, I will move to new locations and slowly start to introduce low distractions (for example, the shopping carts or people) and progress to more difficult distractions (dogs). I will increase the distance from my dog as I want to incorporate all the requirements into every command that is being proofed. Once I have exhausted all possible locations, I will include distance standards as well, looking to achieve an 80% or higher success rate in all tested requirements.

*Pro tip: A great place to train is outside the fence of a dog park. You get a safe, controlled environment with a lot of unpredictability. Another great option for introducing people is standing outside a coffee shop or storefront at a safe distance. The dog gets exposure to the trigger without you having to orchestrate participants.

Before proceeding with the following requirement, I will repeat the bonus step: reassess and test.

Part 3

Step 5: Let's go the extra mile (Duration)

This step of the process brings us to the last D of the three Ds of dog training with Duration. This is where we want to get our dog to hold onto the behavior for a fixed time. This is important because we want to make sure we have control of the dog and teach it to wait for our next instructions or guidance. Some of the key elements of duration are delaying the delivery of rewards and maintaining focus. If this step is missed, the dog might end the command prematurely or, worse, get distracted and blow off the command entirely. This is why following through with every command that is given is crucial for setting the expectation with your dog from day one.

Using our example of the 'sit' command, I will start in my no-distraction environment and prompt for the 'sit' command. Once my dog complies, I will immediately reinforce with the verbal marker, but delay the delivery of the reward, starting with 1 or 2 seconds to start. I will gradually increase the delay by increments of 2 seconds or so. As I achieve an 80% or higher success rate, I will change locations until I have exhausted every location that might be in my dog's life. Slowly I will start to introduce distractions and other requirements while changing locations, in this case, the shopping cart, person, or dog. I set a goal of about 5 to 10 seconds for my dog to be patient and wait for the next instructions. This is almost like an unspoken or non-prompted hold command at the end of a behavior.

Before proceeding with the following requirement, I will repeat the bonus step: reassess and test.

Step 6: Tailored for perfection (Precision)

We are close to wrapping up the 'proofing' of a reliable 'sit' command with our dog. Precision is the standard of what the actual behavior should look like. I want to take this time to say that this is the most subjective part of the 'proofing' process. Everyone has a minimum standard for behaviors given their lifestyle. If you have a dog that is training for

Part 3

competitions, a type of job, this might be more important to you than to others. If you just want a good dog with reliable behaviors and a lazy sit is okay, then so be it. Just make sure that before you even train the behavior, you have an ideal model for the behavior you are trying to achieve, and you don't change it (see Fig. 2 below). I will admit that with my companion dogs, I'm a bit more lenient on how behaviors should be, except for my essential commands. In this example, I have my dog ready to do the sit, making minor adjustments as needed. I use techniques like shaping and capturing to address any flawed areas, again starting in a no-distraction environment. Rewards are given for small progress toward the ideal behavior. The reward schedule changes to reward only correct or precise displays of the behavior once the behavior has been achieved.

Pro Tip: Using high value treats for the behavioral standard helps communicate what is being asked of the dog in this phase of proofing.

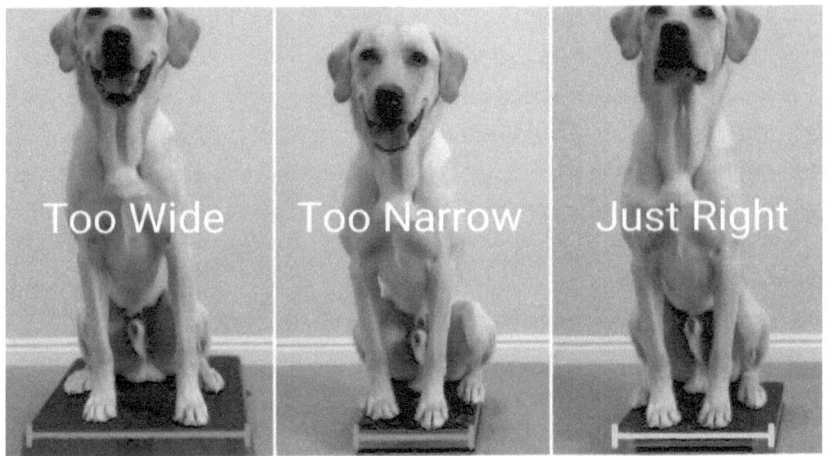

Fig 2

Other tools can be used, like a sit box to mold the position of the 'sit' as seen above in fig 2. As the dog starts to display the proper behavior, I slowly incorporate the other requirements and change location as needed with the same 80% success rate as before.

Part 3

As I mentioned before, where to start in the 'proofing' wheel is entirely up to you, and depending on the behavior, I might choose to start at a different requirement. Precision is one of my alternative starting places for some behaviors.

Before proceeding with the following requirement, I will repeat the bonus step: reassess and test.

Step 7: Race to the end

Applaud yourself for making it to the last step of the proofing wheel, speed. This step is almost a repeat of the latency process with some minor differences. I won't go into grave detail because the process is the same however, the measure of time is from the start of the behavior to the end of the behavior. The critical aspect of this phase is the same, which is the timing, making sure that you are prepared to dish out treats or initiate games that will keep your dog engaged after the behavior has been completed. This time can vary depending on the behavior; however, what does apply is the sense of urgency. I will deviate a bit by using a different behavior as an example for this analogy. In most cases, with a recall command, the dog has two modes: to slowly mosey over and take its time or bolt to you like a freight train without brakes. The standard is the ladder in this case.

Using 'Sit' to stay consistent, I will prep my dog by getting it to a high drive state and encourage fast completion through a timing and reward schedule that influences a faster response. This could also mean more urgency prompting from me as the handler. Once my dog has achieved the standard rate of success of 80% in the initial no-distraction environment, slowly move to new locations with the introduction of distractions and increased distance, duration, and decreased latency requirements.

Before determining a behavior is proofed, I will repeat the bonus step: reassess and test. This time in all areas, under real world conditions at random.

Part 3

That does it for proofing the behavior of 'sit,' we made it to the end, and now you can rinse and repeat as much as you like with new goals set. I imagine that a lot of this sounds tedious, grueling, and most of all time-consuming. That is the very essence of proofing, deliberate, consistent, and intentional. To get a stimulus to become generalized or neutral, overexposure is needed. This very framework ensures that if you follow it step by step without taking shortcuts or trying to fast-track success. I will summarize the process below:

Overview:

Proofing Sit behavior

Step 1: Setting a Goal and Identifying Challenges

Task: Set intention and goal, identify triggers and response.

Accomplish: Assessing the threshold to triggers

Step 2: Exposure and Repetition (distraction)

Goal: Reduce threshold from trigger (i.e., stationary cart) to less than 1 ft while complying with 'sit' command.

Accomplish: Generalizing and overexposure to trigger

Location: starting low-distraction environment then gradually increasing and changing location

Part 3

Bonus step: Reassess and test

Step 3: Increasing Distance

Goal: Increase the distance between the dog and the handler to 10ft, while the shopping cart is near, and complying with the 'sit' command

Accomplish: 80% success rate of sit

Location: no distraction environment then gradually increasing and changing location

Bonus step: Reassess and test

Step 4: Race to the Start (latency)

Goal: Reduce the time between the 'sit' command prompt is given and the start of behavior to within 2 seconds

Accomplish: Faster response time

Location: no distraction environment then gradually increasing and changing location

Bonus step: Reassess and test

Step 5: Let's go the extra mile (Duration)

Goal: Increase focus time after 'sit' behavior to 5 to 10 seconds

Accomplish: dog waiting in 'sit' for additional instruction

Part 3

Location: no distraction environment then gradually increasing and changing location

Bonus step: Reassess and test

Step 6: Tailored for Perfection

Goal: Achieve the standard position of the 'sit' command

Accomplish: Standard of 'sit' behavior when prompted

Location: no distraction environment then gradually increasing and changing location

Bonus step: Reassess and test

Step 7: Race to the End

Goal: Achieve urgency for completion of the 'sit' behavior

Accomplish: Immediacy with completion of 'sit' behavior within 2 seconds

Location: no-distraction environment then gradually increasing and changing location

Bonus step: Reassess and test

Proofing Completed

That's the complete framework, which can be repeated with any behavior, changing the location and trigger until your dog has been exposed to every variety of triggers, location, and prompted to do a desired behavior. I could have swapped out the shopping cart for people or dogs, or changed the behavior to a 'stay,' or 'no barking.' I follow this proofing process with all my personal and clients' dogs. I have included a sample "proofing

Part 3

worksheet" for you to fill out and try at home with your dog. Things to remember. Keep the goal and intention clear for each training session, with a maximum of 20 minutes at most. Slowly and deliberately move through the proofing wheel completely before moving to a new location. Gradually increase the difficulty of the requirements at your dog's pace. It's a good idea to do refresher sessions once you accomplish an objective to ensure it sticks. For example, my dog sits 1ft away from carts without negatively responding. I will do a few more sessions to make sure it's not a fluke and generalize this new threshold before adding need distractions like moving the cart or people. That's proofing in a nutshell. The nuts and bolts of bomb proofing behaviors and battle testing them in real-world scenarios.

Proofing Worksheet

Dog's Name: _____

Trainer/Handler: _____

Command Being Proofed: _____

Date Started: _____

Environment (e.g., park, living room, café):

Step 1: Define Your Goal
What should this command look like in a real-life setting?
Example: Hold a sit-stay at a café while dogs and people pass by until released.

Training Goal:

Part 3

Step 2: Identify Known Triggers & Threshold Distances

Trigger/Distraction	Reaction (bark, break, ignore, etc.)	Threshold Distance (ft)

_____

_____

_____

_____

Step 3: Proofing Wheel Evaluation

Use this chart to track how well your dog is doing in each proofing category.

Proofing Element	Notes on Progress / Challenges	Success Rate (%)	Date
Distraction			
Distance			
Latency			

Part 3

Duration			
Precision			
Speed			

Step 4: Plan for the Next Session

Focus Area(s) Needing Improvement:

Adjustments or Tools to Use:

How Will You Increase Difficulty?
(e.g., add distractions, increase distance or duration)

Step 5: Milestone Check

Mark off when each milestone is achieved:
80%+ success rate across 3+ environments
Maintains behavior under high distraction
Holds behavior at increasing distances

- Responds quickly and accurately (low latency + high precision)
- Consistent performance without leash or prompts (if safe/applicable)

Trainer Notes / Observations:

Part 3

Field Test Commands

This is the final section of the book. I want to share some last-minute stories and words of encouragement as you continue your dog ownership journey. My intention with writing this book was to provide a simple, easy-to-follow anyone can do it guide to dog training. If you have made it to the end of the book, you have been provided with tools to apply to any behavior. However, this is just one perspective and opinion on how things should be done. I highly recommend always seeking professional dog training help when dealing with advanced methods or behaviors. The goal of this book was to provide a framework that could be customized and shaped to anyone's lifestyle, molded to your training style, and adapted to your dog. Dog training is about being creative, flexible, and innovative. So, what better way to put that to the test? Get out there and train, fully embrace the journey and joys that having a dog provides. I have great memories of all the wonderful experiences dog ownership has given me. Dogs provide unconditional love, but also life lessons along the way. I have seen clients gain self-confidence and a newfound purpose in their furry companions. I have seen countless transformations of young kids learning responsibility and accountability through dog ownership. I have seen family's bond over the joy of training their dog. So go out there and field test every command, think outside of the box, and try something new. If you ask three dog trainers how to teach a dog to 'sit', they will give you three different answers and disagree with one another. However, they can agree that the other trainer is doing it wrong. Despite my experience, my success, and my love for training dogs, I will always stand by the idea that the most professional person in your dog's life is you. You understand every little detail and quirk your dog has; you are well-versed in everything Fido.

Now go on and experience every walk, run, hike, and beach that you can. Get out there and volunteer with a rescue group or shelter. Maybe even organizing a pack walk and making some friends, the possibilities are truly endless. I could tell one more story about Onyx and Omni. No, I think I have talked about my girls enough. I hope that you all got a

Part 3

glimpse of just how much they meant to me. This book is a dedication to all the time they put up with me while I became a dog trainer. I know I got a lot of it wrong, but I also got some of it right. I will tell you about Nala, a client's puppy of mine whom I will never forget. The owners of Nala were wonderful and devoted dog owners. They loved Nala a lot and put in time and effort to make sure that she was the best dog that she could be. The mom didn't stop short of getting every resource, training aid, training book, treat, and toy that she could find. She wanted to make sure that Nala had the best life. The owners were first-time pet parents; they had never owned a dog in their adult lives or their relationship. Despite being total newbies, they had dived right into loving and training Nala from 8 weeks old, day one of bringing her home. Nala was a King Charles Spaniel and cute as a button. She was a very sweet dog, loved cuddles, and taking pictures. I got the honor of seeing Nala grow from an excited puppy to an adolescent dog who was learning new behaviors week by week.

We always must accept the good with the bad, and unfortunately, this story doesn't end with Nala becoming a world champion in obedience or rally. It doesn't end with her biting a kid and having to be put down. It does have a sad ending, but a lesson that taught me just how precious time will always be. I remember having to drive an hour one way to do my lessons for Nala and her parents, I was invested in their success. So, after we had completed roughly 3 or 4 lessons of the 6, they had purchased at the time. I got a call one evening. It was Nala's mom calling to tell me that she wanted to discontinue the lessons. The reason was not because she was unhappy with my service, nope, nothing like that. It was because she got bad news that 6-month-old Nala wouldn't make it to her 1-year birthday. Nala had a condition that would cut her life short. Nala's mom wanted to take what she had learned and give Nala the best last few months of her life. I remember learning that dog trainers get the joy of playing with puppies and cuddling with dogs about 80% of the time. We also have 10% of dogs that want to bite us or might be stubborn. However, it's that last 10% that no one tells you about before you fall in love with the profession. It's the ones that you lose that you never forget.

Part 3

That moment I learned that I get to share success stories, I get to see dogs and humans connect and become a team through training. However, I also witnessed the training from potty pads to potty diapers and witnessed the grief of the families mourning the loss of their family members. That was the day I cried because it felt like I lost one of my dogs. So, for the memory of Nala and all the other dogs we've lost, go out and walk your dog and tell them about your day. Cuddle up with them while you watch Netflix. Let them tag along for the Starbucks run and treat them to a PUP-puccino. However, most importantly, get out and train your dog.

I titled the book "I like my dog until I don't" because it's true— we all get frustrated with our pups. They come to terrorize the house, destroy the yard and sofa, and don't get me started on the $200 pair of shoes they shred to pieces. Yet even when we don't always like our dogs, we will always love our dogs.

Thank you for reading and for sharing in the joys (and chaos) of dog ownership.

Afterword

If you've made it to this page, thank you. Thank you for your time, your trust, and your willingness to grow—not just as a dog owner, but as a leader, a guide, and a partner to your dog.

This book wasn't written from a tower. It was written from the floor—literally. Sitting on dog beds, wrestling in backyards, cleaning up accidents, and learning the hard way, one mistake and one victory at a time. What you've read here isn't theory pulled from textbooks—it's lived experience. It's the stuff that happens when you love your dog enough to keep showing up, even when you're tired, frustrated, or unsure.

I've said this before, but it's worth repeating: the most professional person in your dog's life is you. Not your local trainer. Not the books or YouTube videos. Not even me. Your dog doesn't care about credentials; they care about consistency, patience, and presence. They care about the human who gets down on the floor with them, makes eye contact, and says, "I'm in this with you."

Throughout this book, I've shared the stories of Onyx, Omni, and Nala—three very different dogs who shaped me in powerful ways. Onyx taught me about boundaries and the importance of reading behavior early. Omni taught me that progress is sometimes slow, and consistency beats quick wins. Nala showed me how joy and energy, when paired with structure, can create something beautiful. Each of them helped me become the trainer—and the person—I am today.

If there's one message I want you to walk away with, it's this: training never ends. It evolves. The best relationships, just like the best-trained dogs, are built over time with daily intention. This

Afterword

process isn't about perfection. It's about showing up. It's about doing the work with empathy and clarity, knowing that your dog is always learning—even when you think they aren't. You don't need to have all the answers. You just need to be willing. Every interaction, every walk, every feeding, every game—that's training. That's bonding. And when things feel hard—and they will—remind yourself of why you started. Come back to the trust you're building, not the task list you're checking off. I hope this book has made you feel seen as a dog owner. I hope it's made you laugh, reflect, and maybe even shift the way you see your dog—and yourself. Whether you're just starting or you've been doing this for years, remember: your dog isn't looking for perfect. They're looking for *you*.

Thank you for letting me be part of your journey. Close this book, grab the leash, and get back to the real work, the kind that builds a bond your dog will never forget.

With appreciation and respect,
Aaron A. Lee

In Loving Memory of Nala

Forever in our hearts
Thank you, Nala, for every wag, every lesson, and every moment of joy
you brought. You were a companion, a friend, and a bright spirit. You will
always be remembered and forever missed.

Worksheets and Training Tools

Continue Your Training Journey

If this book helped you and your dog build something better, don't stop here. You can keep using the tools I've made for you — all free, all designed to work in real life.

✔ Printable worksheets

✔ Hand signal visuals in full color

✔ Walkthrough videos of the drills

✔ Bonus content and updates from me as I keep learning too

🔗 **https://bit.ly/ilikemydogbookresources**
Scan the QR code below to access your free tools.

🌐 Learn More

Find group classes, private training, and additional programs at:
PawfectPractice.training

You and your dog are capable of amazing things — keep going!

🐾 Recall 101: Foundation Without Cue

Training Goal:
Ex: Teach the foundational behavior of recall before introducing a verbal cue.

Training Environment:
☐ Enclosed Space
☐ Low/No Distractions
☐ Safety Checked

Tools Needed:
☐ 6 ft Leash
☐ High-Value Rewards (treats, toys, tug)

✅ SESSION CHECKLIST

Warm-Up (2–3 min):
☐ Social play engaged (tug, chase, name game)
☐ Dog is on leash
☐ Dog shows interest/focus.

Drill 1 (3–5 min):
☐ Handler applies gentle leash pressure
☐ Dog commits to movement → pressure released
☐ Handler prompts a sit (no recall cue used)
☐ Mark with "Yes" and maintain eye contact (2–3 sec)
☐ Reward delivered.

Disengage (1–2 min):

☐ Walk around or use a helper to create distance

☐ Dog voluntarily disengages.

Drill 2 (Repeat of above):

☐ Apply leash pressure again

☐ Dog commits → pressure released

☐ Prompt, sit, mark, reward.

Cooldown (2 min):

☐ End with 2–3 known cues (e.g., sit, name game)

☐ Positive tone maintained.

Observations:

How many successful repetitions did the dog complete? _____

What was the dog's reaction to leash pressure? _____

Any hesitation or confusion? _____

Next goal (e.g., build confidence, reduce latency):

💡 *Pro tip*: No verbal cue yet. Let the dog learn through shaping using rewards and timing.

⁂ Recall 400: Advanced Long-Distance Recall

Training Goal:
Ex: Recall up to 50 ft with low distractions

Training Environment:
☐ Enclosed Area or Fenced Field
☐ Low-Medium Distractions (e.g., toys on the ground)
☐ Dog is trained on cue and has foundation.

Tools Needed:
☐ 50 ft Long Line
☐ High-Value Rewards (treats, toys, tug)

☑ SESSION CHECKLIST

Warm-Up (2–3 min):
☐ Social play or name game (on or off leash depending on dog)
☐ Dog engaged and ready.

Drill 1 (3–5 min):
☐ Dog is ~50 ft away
☐ Handler applies leash pressure + verbal encouragement
☐ Dog commits → release pressure
☐ When dog is within 10 ft, give recall cue
☐ Dog returns → mark & eye contact (2–3 sec), reward

Disengage (1–2 min):
☐ Dog allowed to walk away
☐ Optional second person engages to create space.

Drill 2 (2–3 min):

☐ Repeat drill

☐ Include mild distractions (toys/treats on floor)

☐ Handler uses verbal recall only if behavior is fluent.

Cooldown (2 min):

☐ End session with familiar cues (sit, name, focus)

☐ Reward and praise to maintain positive tone.

Observations:

Distance prompted: _____ ft

Success rate (out of 5 reps): _____

Distractions ignored: ☐ Yes ☐ No

Did leash pressure become unnecessary? ☐ Yes ☐ No

Next training target (e.g., higher distraction, no leash):

_____

 Pro Tip: Never call your dog to punish. Recall must always predict something good.

🐾 Drop it 101: The Basics

Training Goal:
Ex: Set the foundation for the "Drop it" command in a safe, controlled environment.

Methods Used:

- Luring
- Capturing
- Positive Reinforcement

Training Tools:

- Preferred toy
- Preferred treat
- Long line (15 ft)

🔧 Setup Checklist

☐ Training area free of hazards

☐ Long line securely attached

☐ Toy and treats ready (treats hidden from view)

☐ Planned distractions noted: _____

📋 Training Steps

1. Social Play (2–3 min)

☐ Play tug with your dog to build engagement

☐ Ensure the dog is wearing the long line

2. Intro to Drop – Luring (3–5 min)

☐ Continue tug

☐ Freeze the toy

☐ Present a hidden treat—reward when the dog lets go

☐ Repeat as needed

☐ ☐ Skip if ground drop is not your behavior goal

3. Drop to Ground – Luring (3–5 min)

☐ Tug > freeze > treat presented

☐ Let the toy fall to the ground

☐ Mark and reward when the dog drops the toy

☐ Repeat

☐ ☐ Skip if hand-delivery is the behavior goal

4. Add Verbal Cue (3–5 min)

☐ Repeat step 2 or 3

☐ Before treat, say "Drop it" or "Hand"

☐ Mark and reward when behavior is performed

☐ Repeat several times

5. Tug as Reward (3–5 min)

☐ Prompt behavior

☐ Mark when completed

☐ Reward by resuming the tug instead of a treat

6. End with a Win

☐ Let the dog win the final round of tug

💡 Pro Tip

You can teach both:

- "Drop it" = Let go on the floor

"Hand" = Place the item in your hand

🐾 Drop it 350: Drop it with Distance

Training Goal:
Ex: Teach your dog to respond to the "Drop it" cue at a distance.
(Not applicable for "Hand" command)

Methods Used:

- Shaping
- Positive reinforcement

Training Tools:

- Preferred toy
- Preferred treat

🛠 Setup Checklist

☐ Controlled, distraction-aware environment
☐ Long line attached
☐ Toys and treats are ready
☐ Planned distractions noted: _____

This exercise focuses on the reliability of the "Drop it" cue when the handler is not nearby. Rewards should be given on a variable schedule to strengthen behavior.

📋 Training Steps

1. Social Play (2–3 min)
☐ Play tug with your dog to build focus and motivation
☐ Ensure the dog is on a long line

2. Drop it from Distance (3–5 min)

☐ Tug, then release the toy and give the "Drop it" cue

☐ Mark the correct response and deliver a reward

☐ Repeat several times

☐ Use a **variable reward schedule** — e.g., reward after 1, 3, then 2 drops

☐   Skip this step if training "Hand" behavior

---

3. Drop into Hand (3–5 min)

☐ Tug > let go of toy > present open hand

☐ Prompt with "Hand"

☐ Mark and reward appropriate response

☐ Use a variable reward schedule

☐   Skip this step if the training ground drops only

---

4. Repeat for Practice (3–5 min)

☐ Continue with your preferred training version (step 2 or 3)

☐ Focus on consistency and engagement

---

5. Tug as Reward (3–5 min)

☐ Prompt desired behavior

☐ Mark success

☐ Reward by restarting the tug game rather than using a treat

6. End with a Win

☐ Let your dog win the final round of tug

 Pro Tip

A **slot machine-style reward system** (random and varied) helps build stronger behavior that doesn't rely on constant treats. Dogs work harder for a reward that's not guaranteed every time.

🐾 Leave It 101: Building the Foundation

Training Goal:
Ex: Teach the dog to disengage from a low-value reward and give attention to the handler.

Methods: Shaping, positive reinforcement, leash pressure (as needed)

Tools Needed: Leash, high-value reward, lower-value bait treat.

Training Environment:
☐ Controlled space
☐ Safety checked
☐ Distraction level: ☐ None ☐ Low ☐ Medium

✅ SESSION FLOW

1. Warm-Up (2–3 min)
☐ Social play (tug, chase, name game)
☐ Dog is engaged and on leash

---

2. Choose Method & Execute Drill (3–5 min)
Select ONE method for the session:

☐ **Hand Method** – Cover bait with open fingers

☐ **Foot Method** – Hover foot over the bait treat

☐ **Leash Method** – Toss bait just outside leash range

☐ Encourage the dog's interest in the bait treat

☐ Redirect the dog's attention using sound or leash pressure

☐ When dog gives eye contact → mark ("Yes") → deliver high-value reward

3. Repeat (3–5 min)

☐ Repeat redirection and marking ~10 reps

☐ Encourage the dog's attention back to the bait each time

☐ Maintain consistency with your sound/timing

---

4. Add Verbal Cue (3–5 min)

☐ Begin saying "Leave it" as the dog approaches the bait

☐ If needed, reinforce with sound or leash pressure

☐ Eye contact → mark → reward

☐ Repeat until the cue is associated with the behavior

---

5. Cooldown & Close (2 min)

☐ End with a known cue (e.g., sit or successful leave it)

☐ Remove all bait treats—**never let the dog access them**

📑 Session Notes

Which method did you use today? _____

Session of successful "leave it" redirections: _____

- Was leash pressure needed? ☐ Yes ☐ No

- Did the dog respond to the cue alone? ☐ Yes ☐ No

Distractions noticed? _____

Next session goal: _____

💡 *Pro Tip*: Use a "jackpot" reward (several treats in a row) to make reinforcement more powerful.

🐾 Leave it 350: Advanced Leave it Training

Training Goal:

*Ex: Teach your dog to reliably respond to the **"Leave it"** cue, even off leash.*

Methods Used:

- Positive reinforcement
- Negative reinforcement
- Leash pressure
- Shaping

Training Tools:

- Preferred treat
- Decoy reward
- Long line (15 ft)

🪓 Setup Checklist

☐ Safe, controlled training space

☐ Long line attached

☐ Decoy rewards are placed 3–4 ft apart

☐ Preferred treats prepared

☐ Planned distractions noted: _____

Use decoys like plastic containers with perforations to prevent access. Place them along a path to shape calm behavior. Later, replace it with open treats on the ground.

📋 **Training Steps**

1. Social Play (2–3 min)

☐ Begin with a game of tug

☐ Focus on engagement and attention

☐ The dog should be wearing a long line

---

2. Introduce Decoy – Leashed Walk (3–5 min)

☐ Set up 3–4 decoy treat containers in a linear path

☐ Walk past with your dog on a leash

☐ When the dog notices a decoy, say "Leave it."

☐ Mark and reward when the dog disengages

☐ Gradually reduce the distance to decoys

---

3. Repeat Sessions (1–2 min per trial)

☐ Conduct multiple short sessions

☐ Maintain a high success rate before advancing

☐ Reinforce consistency before increasing difficulty

---

4. Free Treat Challenge (Multiple sessions)

☐ Replace decoys with openly placed treats

☐ Begin with wide spacing

☐ Use "Leave it" cue as dog approaches

☐ Mark and reward the correct response

☐ Gradually decrease spacing as the dog succeeds

☐ Be patient — progress may take time

5. End the Session (2 min)

☐ Finish with a basic command like "Sit."

☐ Remove all treats and decoys from the area

☐ Never let the dog retrieve the decoys after "Leave it" is prompted

---

 Pro Tip

Use **different materials** for decoys as the dog improves (e.g., toys, varied treats, scents). This enhances generalization and real-world reliability.

❧ Stay and Wait 101: The Basics of Holding Positions

Training Goal:

Ex: Introduce and build foundation for the "Stay" and "Wait" commands with low distractions.

Methods Used:

- Positive reinforcement
- Capturing

Training Tools:

- Dog's preferred reward
- Leash or long line
- Cot or bed (optional)

🛠 Setup Checklist

☐ Enclosed, quiet training space
☐ Leash or long line attached
☐ Treats or toys ready for reward
☐ Cot/bed in position (if using)
☐ Distractions minimized or removed

The "stay" and "wait" commands teach impulse control and position holding. Success starts with timing, repetition, and working within your dog's threshold.

📝 Training Steps

1. Social Play Warm-up (2–3 min)

☐ Use light play (name game, tug, or chase) to focus your dog

☐ Keep leash or long line attached for proximity and control

2. Sit + Eye Contact Duration (3–5 min)

☐ Prompt your dog to sit

☐ Mark with **"Yes"** and maintain eye contact

☐ If needed, hold a treat in view without giving it

☐ Mark again and reward after a short hold

☐ Encourage a reset and repeat

☐ Gradually increase the duration of the sit-hold

3. Begin Movement Challenge (1–2 min)

☐ Ask for a sit again

☐ Slowly move one foot back while giving a stop-hand gesture

☐ Encourage the dog to stay by holding eye contact

☐ Repeat while increasing to a full step away

4. Verbal + Hand Cue Pairing (Multiple sessions)

☐ Reset with some movement

☐ Prompt to sit again

☐ Pair **"Stay"** with a stop-hand gesture

☐ Hold for just 1–2 seconds

☐ Mark with **"Good"**, then say **"Release"** and give a reward

☐ Repeat over sessions, building both **duration** and **distance**

5. End the Session (2 min)

☐ Finish with familiar cues like "Sit" or name recall

☐ Maintain a calm, celebratory tone to reinforce learning

💡 Pro Tip

Using a **cot or raised surface** can add visual boundaries, making it easier for your dog to understand when to stay and when to release.

🐾 Stay and Wait 301: The Advanced Holding Positions

Training Goal:

*Ex: Advance your dog's ability to **"Stay"** and **"Wait"** with distractions and distance.*

Methods Used:

- Positive reinforcement
- Capturing

Training Tools:

- Dog's preferred reward
- Leash or long line
- Cot or bed (optional)

🛠 Setup Checklist

☐ Enclosed training area with controlled distractions

☐ Long line or leash attached

☐ Rewards prepared

☐ Cot/bed available (optional)

☐ Planned distractions noted: _____

This exercise builds on earlier foundation work, gradually increasing both the distance and duration of holds, while integrating distractions to improve reliability.

📋 **Training Steps**

1. Social Play Warm-up (2–3 min)
☐ Use tug, chase, or the name game to build engagement
☐ Keep leash or long line on for control and focus

---

2. Intro to Distance and Duration (3–5 min)
☐ Prompt a sit and give the **"Stay"** cue
☐ Mark with **"Yes"** and maintain eye contact
☐ Take 1–2 steps back; if your dog holds, mark again with **"Good"**
☐ Return to deliver the treat, then say **"Release."**
☐ Repeat, gradually increasing steps and time

💡 **Pro Tip:**
Holds are the exception to the "say it once" rule — it's okay to repeat your stay/wait cue to remind your dog.

---

3. Increase Distance with Reminders (2–5 min)
☐ Prompt **Sit-Stay** again
☐ Take more steps away — mark with **"Good"** during the hold
☐ Use a reminder cue partway through if needed
☐ Return and mark with **"Good stay"**, deliver a reward
☐ Say **"Release"** and reset
☐ Repeat over multiple trials, slowly increasing difficulty with distance or light distractions

4. Close the Session (2 min)

☐ End on a strong note using familiar commands like "Sit" or the name game

☐ Keep it light and positive — success matters more than difficulty

---

 **Pro Tip**

Gradual **layering of distractions** (such as toys, sounds, or movement) helps solidify the behavior. Return to easier steps when introducing something new.

🐾 Loose Leash Walking 101: The Basics

Training Goal:

*Ex: Introduce **leash communication** and build the foundation for polite leash walking.*

Methods Used:

- Luring
- Shaping
- Positive reinforcement

Training Tools:

- 6 ft leash
- Dog's preferred reward (treats, toys, or tug)

🛠 Setup Checklist

☐ Start in a low-distraction environment (e.g., backyard)
☐ The leash and reward are ready
☐ Dog exercised briefly beforehand
☐ Walk scheduled before feeding for increased treat motivation

*Focus on **quality over distance**. Training walks are split into three phases and should be repeated daily.*

⚚ Training Phases

Phase 1: Social Play and Engagement (2–3 min)

☐ Engage with your dog using tug, chase, or the name game

☐ Build energy and focus while on leash

☐ This phase helps reduce excess energy before walking

Phase 2: Training (3–5 min per step)

2. Structured Walking Start

☐ Begin with your dog in a sit at your walking side

☐ Say your dog's name + "Let's go" as you move forward

☐ Lure with treats to keep proper walking position (shoulder to mid-body)

☐ Reward while walking and when you stop, cue a sit → mark → reward

☐ Repeat with varied step counts

---

3. Walking Patterns & Attention Building

☐ Use shapes like ovals, figure 8s, and squares

☐ Vary walking speed (slow → fast, fast → slow)

☐ Lure through turns, gradually fade the lure

☐ Reward using increasing intervals:

• Every odd number (1, 3, 5...)

• Every 3 steps → 5 steps → only at stops

☙ Pro Tip:

Expect frequent corrections and redirections early on. Review drills and troubleshooting in the *Worksheets & Tools* section later in the book.

Phase 3: Leisure Walk (1–2 min)

☐ Allow sniffing and "dog time" on leash

☐ Use as a **reward phase** for good walking during training

Progression and Repetition

4. Repeat Sessions Regularly

☐ Run phases 1–3 multiple times per day

☐ Gradually introduce distractions as your dog improves

☐ Always stay within your dog's current threshold and adjust difficulty slowly

5. Close the Session (2 min)

☐ End with familiar cues like "Sit" or name recognition

☐ Keep the tone positive to reinforce success

🔄 **Weekly Goal:**

Practice consistently, layering in difficulty slowly and reinforcing every improvement with praise and patience.

🐾 Loose Leash Walking 301: Advanced Leash Walking

Training Goal:
*Ex: Teach **leash walking with distractions and integrated commands** in real-world* environments.

Methods Used:

- Luring
- Shaping
- Positive reinforcement

Training Tools:

- 6 ft leash
- Dog's preferred reward (treats, toys, or tug)

🏹 Setup Checklist

☐ Moderate-distraction environment (e.g., neighborhood, store, or park)
☐ Leash and rewards prepared
☐ The dog is lightly exercised beforehand
☐ Walk scheduled before feeding for stronger treat motivation
☐ Planned distractions noted: _____

*At this level, we prioritize **consistency and responsiveness** while gradually reducing the need for lures and corrections.*

🧍 Training Phases

Phase 1: Social Play and Engagement (2–3 min)

☐ Use light play (chase, tug, or name game) on leash to build focus
☐ Maintain calm excitement and connection before starting the walk

---

Phase 2: Advanced Leash Training (3–5 min)

2. Leash Communication with Distractions

☐ Begin with a sit at your side, facing forward
☐ Say your dog's name + "Let's go" and begin walking
☐ Do not use a lure — gain focus with your voice
☐ Reward correct position (shoulder to mid-body) while walking
☐ At stops, your dog should sit automatically → mark, → reward
☐ Repeat with varied distances and environmental distractions

💡 Pro Tip:

At this stage, **correction and redirection should be rare**. Use subtle leash pressure or verbal cues as needed.

Phase 3: Leisure Phase (1–2 min)

☐ Allow your dog to sniff and explore within leash limits
☐ Use this as a **built-in reward** for good leash behavior

Progression and Repetition

4. Repeat Sessions with Increasing Distractions

☐ Revisit phases 1–3 across multiple sessions

☐ Gradually increase the challenge of your environment

☐ Monitor thresholds and reduce difficulty if the dog loses focus

5. Close the Session (2 min)

☐ Use familiar cues like "Sit," "Name," or "Look" to finish

☐ Maintain a positive tone and consistent structure

🦌 **Weekly Goal** - Strive for **autopilot leash behavior** in moderately busy environments. Reinforce calm walking, timely 'sits', and responsive engagement.

 Drop (Stop) 401: The Basics

Training Goal:

Ex: Establish a reliable foundation for the "Drop" or "Stop" cue without distractions.

Methods Used:

- Shaping
- Luring
- Positive reinforcement

Training Tools:

- Long line (15 ft recommended)
- Dog's preferred reward (treats, toys, or tug)

🪓 Setup Checklist

☐ Safe, enclosed training area
☐ Long line securely attached
☐ Treats or toys prepared
☐ Distraction-free environment
☐ Gradual progression plan in place

This command teaches the dog to stop and lie down instantly, a critical skill for safety and advanced control.

📋 Training Steps

1. Social Play Warm-up (2–3 min)
☐ Engage in tug, chase, or recall games

☐ Keep the dog on a leash or long line to maintain connection and focus

2. Down from a Distance (3–5 min)

☐ From standing, cue "Down" → mark → reward

☐ Repeat until consistent

☐ Begin adding distance (2–3 ft → up to 20 ft)

☐ Prompt from farther away → mark → reward

☐ Build gradual fluency over several sessions

3. Drop While Moving (3–5 min)

☐ Walk with your dog at your side

☐ Mid-walk, cue "Drop"

☐ If needed, pair with "Down" until the dog understands

☐ Remove lure over time and mark + reward responses

☐ Repeat at a faster pace for momentum control

Variation:

☐ Walk backward as your dog walks toward you

☐ Stop → cue "Drop"

☐ Later, step forward slightly to block movement

☐ Mark and reward appropriate responses

4. Barrier Training (Optional – 3–5 min)

☐ Place a broomstick or PVC pipe between you and your dog

☐ Cue "Down" when dog reaches barrier

☐ Toss treat behind dog to create space, then cue again as they return

☐ Use sparingly and fade the barrier over time

5. Drop on Recall (3–5 min)

☐ From 3 ft away, cue a recall, then immediately follow with

"Drop"

☐ If needed, step into the dog's path to create clarity

☐ Repeat this combination over several sessions

☐ Mark + reward the stop, not just the recall

6. Close the Session (2 min)

☐ End with a few known commands like "Sit" or "Look"

☐ Keep closure light, successful, and rewarding

💡 **Pro Tip:** *Your dog's ability to "drop" mid-motion can prevent injury and build serious control. Build distance and difficulty slowly and keep your timing sharp.*

🐾 Drop (Stop) 401: The Advanced Training

Training Goal:

*Ex: Build foundational reliability for the **"Drop"** (or **"Stop"**) cue in low-distraction settings.*

Methods Used:

- Shaping
- Luring
- Positive reinforcement

Training Tools:

- Dog's preferred reward (treats, toys, or tug)
- Long line (15 ft recommended)

🔧 Setup Checklist

☐ Safe, enclosed training area

☐ Long line securely attached

☐ Treats/toys prepared

☐ Environment free from distractions

☐ Target distance goal (up to 20 ft) planned

This command lays the groundwork for emergency stop behavior. Early success depends on clarity, timing, and gradually increased distance.

📋 **Training Steps**

1. Social Play Warm-up (2–3 min)

☐ Start with tug, chase, or recall games

☐ Keep the dog on a leash or long line for safety and engagement

2. Stationary Down + Distance Building (3–5 min)

☐ From a standing position, cue **"Down"** → mark → reward

☐ Repeat until consistent

☐ Begin adding distance: 2–3 ft → Work up to 20 ft

☐ Prompt from a distance → mark → reward

☐ Repeat for consistency

3. Drop While in Motion (3–5 min)

☐ Walk with your dog at your side

☐ Mid-walk, cue **"Drop"**

☐ If needed, briefly lure — then phase out

☐ If unfamiliar, pair with **"Down"** until understood

☐ Next, walk backward while the dog walks toward you

• Stop and cue **"Drop"**

• Later, step forward slightly to block the path for clarity

☐ Mark all correct responses and reward

4. Optional Barrier Training (3–5 min)

☐ Use a broomstick or PVC pipe as a boundary

☐ Prompt **"Down"** when the dog reaches the barrier

☐ Toss treat behind dog → repeat as they return

☐ Only use as a shaping tool — phase out quickly

💡 *Optional step — use only if helpful*

5. Introduce Drop During Recall (3–5 min)

☐ Start with dog 3 ft away

☐ Cue **recall** followed by **"Drop"** mid-movement

☐ Step forward if needed to block the path

☐ Repeat this sequence multiple times over several sessions

6. End the Session (2 min)

☐ Close with known commands like "Sit" or "Look"

☐ Keep energy calm and positive

☐ Reinforce engagement before releasing the dog

♡ Pro Tip

The "Drop" cue is life-saving when proofed and reliable. Be consistent with rewards, and don't rush the distance or distractions too early. Building fluency takes time.

✻ Drop (Stop) 410: The Advanced Drop Command

Training Goal:

Ex: Teach reliable "Drop" or "Stop" from a distance with distractions.

Methods Used:

- Shaping
- Luring
- Positive reinforcement

Training Tools:

- Dog's preferred reward (treats, toys, or tug)

🛠 Setup Checklist

☐ Enclosed space with controlled, safe distractions

☐ Rewards ready

☐ Off-leash environment (dog must already be responsive)

☐ Known distraction source available (person, dog, etc.)

☐ Distance and difficulty plan outlined

This level reinforces impulse control with distractions. Be patient — high-level obedience takes repetition and precise timing.

---

1. Social Play Warm-up (2–3 min)

☐ Engage in fun, active play with your dog off-leash

☐ Tug, chase, or name game to focus attention before work begins

2. Reintroduce Drop with Light Distractions (3–5 min)

☐ Begin with a few successful "Drop" trials at your current

working distance

☐ Introduce a light distraction (person or calm dog at a distance)

☐ Prompt "Drop" → mark → reward

☐ Repeat until consistent before progressing

3. Distance Before Distraction (3–5 min)

☐ Remove distractions temporarily

☐ Increase working distance

☐ Run several trials of "Drop" at the new range

☐ Reintroduce prior distraction at a distance

☐ Repeat drop trials while reinforcing focus

4. Distraction Closer to Path (3–5 min)

☐ Gradually move the distraction nearer to your dog's path

☐ If the dog fails, reset by increasing the distance from the distraction

☐ Repeat over several sessions, refining response reliability

5. Generalize with Challenging Distractions (3–5 min)

☐ Continue increasing both distance and distraction intensity

☐ Introduce harder stimuli:
  • Sounds (clapping, jingles)
  • Tossed toys or balls
  • Active dogs in visual range

☐ Reward only for successful, immediate "Drop" responses

☐ Repeat in multiple sessions to reinforce behavior under pressure

6. End the Session (2 min)

☐ Cool down with familiar cues like "Sit" or "Look"

☐ Reinforce connection and success before release

💡 **Pro Tip:** If your dog struggles, scale difficulty back — reduce distance, increase treat value, or soften distractions. The goal is calm precision, not just compliance.

🎯 Dog Training Games & Drills List

🧠 Engagement & Focus Games

1. **Name Game**
   → Reward the dog for looking at you when you say their name. Builds engagement.
2. **Look at That (LAT)**
   → Reward the dog for calmly noticing a trigger or distraction. Teaches neutrality.
3. **Hand Targeting Game (Touch)**
   → The dog boops their nose to your hand. Great for redirection and recall setups.
4. **Focus and Follow**
   → Reward the dog for checking in and choosing to walk with you voluntarily.

🐾 Recall Drills

5. **Chase Me Recall**
   → Run away from the dog, then cue recall. Builds enthusiasm and reliability.
6. **Ping Pong Recall**
   → Two handlers take turns calling the dog between them. Builds speed and fluency.
7. **Hide & Seek**
   → Hide in the house or yard, then call your dog. Reinforces search behavior and recall.
8. **Collar Grab Game**
   → Dog earns rewards for allowing their collar to be held. Prepares for emergencies.

🐕 Leash Skills & Loose-Leash Walking

9. **Silky Leash Drill**
   → Apply light leash pressure and reward for yielding. Builds leash awareness.
10. **Red Light, Green Light**
    → Stop when the dog pulls; move when the leash is slack. Teaches self-control.

11. **Find It Walks**
→ Toss treats slightly ahead during walks. Adds engagement and scent work.

♟ Impulse Control Games

12. **It's Your Choice (IYC)**
→ Offer open hand with treats; the dog learns not to take until released.
13. **Leave It vs. Take It**
→ Present two items (one forbidden). The dog learns to discriminate based on a cue.
14. **Door Manners Game**
→ Teach the dog to sit and wait calmly at doors before being released.
15. **Food Bowl Wait**
→ Dog holds position until released to eat. This builds patience.

◈ Place/Mat Games

16. **Go to Mat**
→ Dog learns to go to a designated spot and stay.
17. **Boundary Games**
→ Reinforce staying within visual or physical boundaries (mat, bed, crate).
18. **Mat to Handler Drill**
→ Send the dog between the mat and you, back and forth. Builds impulse control and fluency.

⌂ Household Skills & Practical Drills

19. **Settle on Cue**
→ Teach the dog to relax on command in a designated spot.
20. **Station Rotation**
→ Practice moving between stations (crate, mat, place). Useful for multi-dog households.
21. **Brush & Treat**
→ Desensitize to grooming by pairing brush strokes with rewards.

22. **Nail Trim Bucket Game**
    → Teach the dog to offer paws and remain still for trims (husbandry behavior).

♀ Enrichment & Play-Based Learning

23. **Find It!**
    → Scatter or hide treats/toys for scent-based fun.
24. **Shell Game**
    → Hide a treat under cups and let the dog sniff out the right one.
25. **Tug & Out Drill**
    → Play tug, then cue "Out" or "Drop It" and reward compliance.
26. **Obstacle Course**
    → Use chairs, tunnels, and cones for a DIY agility circuit.

☜ Advanced Skills Drills

27. **Backup Game**
    → Teach the dog to walk backward on cue. Helps spatial awareness.
28. **Middle (Center Position)**
    → Dog sits or stands between your legs. Great for focus and public work.
29. **Pattern Games (e.g., 1-2-3 Game)**
    → Predictable movement games that help with anxious or reactive dogs.
30. **Directional Send (Left/Right)**
    → Teach the dog to move in specific directions on cue. Useful for sport, agility, or control at a distance.

BONUS DRILL: The Half Dome

A Progressive Proofing Drill Based on the 100 Peck Method

Introduction: Why the Half Dome Works

The Half Dome drill is inspired by the 100 Peck Method, a behavioral training approach originally documented in learning research with pigeons. In the experiment, birds were asked to peck a specific target repeatedly, with the trainer gradually increasing expectations in small increments. The key scientific principle is that successive approximation with extremely small, achievable steps maintains focus, motivation, and precision.

This progression style later influenced duration-building strategies in dog training, especially for stays, distance work, and impulse control. The Half Dome applies these principles directly to help your dog hold a position reliably while you move around them in controlled, systematic steps.

What the Drill Does

1. Builds strong distance control.
2. Strengthens a stay or wait command.
3. Improves your dog's confidence while you move.
4. Creates real-world reliability for sports, obedience, off-leash skills, or therapy dog prep.
5. Makes the behavior extremely consistent because the increments are so gradual.

Handler Setup

- Start with the dog in a sit or down stay (you can also use wait) directly in front of you.
- Stand facing them about one foot away.
- Have high-value treats ready.
- Keep your voice calm and your movements controlled.

Dog Training Games & Drills List

The Rules of the Drill

You are using 100 Peck logic here, meaning you build behavior in tiny, predictable increments. The rules are simple but strict.

1. If the dog breaks position, you restart from Step 1. This teaches the dog that their consistency earns the reward.
2. Increase difficulty only one small unit at a time.
3. End each rep by returning to the dog. The dog should not come to you.
4. Use calm, consistent pacing. Smooth movement keeps the dog regulated.

Phase 1: Straight-Back Distance

Start directly in front of the dog. Take one step back. Return to your starting point and reward. Take two steps back. Return to your starting point and reward. Continue until you reach your target number of steps. I would recommend starting with a basic level of around a 10-step distance. Once you are familiar, try moving up to the more advanced level, up to 20 or more steps in distance.

Remember the first rule of this drill. If the dog breaks for any reason, start back at step 1.

Phase 2: Lateral Movement (The Half Dome)

Once the straight-back distance is solid, begin building a semi-circle around the dog.

Left Side

Begin building the arc by combining backward steps with gradual lateral movement. Take one step back and one small step to the left. Return to your starting point by the same path you took from the dog and reward. Next, take two steps back and two small steps to the left. Return and reward. Continue increasing in these small, steady increments until you have moved far enough left that you are standing on the dog's side, forming the left half of the arc.

*Pro tip: When returning to the dog, take the same path, number of steps to reduce any additional variables from the drill.

Right Side

Repeat the same progression on the opposite side. Start with one step back and one small step to the right, return, reward, then increase to two steps back and two steps to the right, and so on. Continue until you have mirrored the arc on the dog's right side, completing the full half dome around them.

Purpose of the Arc

By the end of the drill, you will have created a spacious semi-circle around your dog. The goal is to eventually move freely anywhere within this half dome while your dog remains in position without breaking the stay. This level of reliability only develops when the handler works **slowly**, follows the progression **rules,** and remains **intentional** with every rep. The gradual build reinforces clarity, confidence, and stability for the dog as the handler's movement becomes more dynamic within the shaped space.

Once you finish the semicircle on one side, reset your dog into a stay facing the opposite direction and build the arc on the other side. This creates a complete 360° training circle. The long-term goal is to move freely anywhere around your dog without them breaking the stay. This usually takes multiple sessions on each side, so go slow, stay consistent, and don't rush the process.

Why This Drill Is Effective

You combine distance, movement, and handler unpredictability in one exercise. You are shaping the dog's ability to hold position despite motion in multiple directions. The restart rule creates clarity and structure. The dog learns to choose stillness even as movement becomes tempting.

Common Mistakes

1. Increasing steps too quickly
2. Talking too much and distracting the dog
3. Rewarding with excitement that breaks the stay
4. Moving too fast or erratically
5. Not resetting all the way to step one after a mistake

Troubleshooting

If the dog keeps breaking at the same distance, maintain that distance for several successful reps before increasing. If the dog breaks during lateral movement, your steps are probably too big. Use smaller increments. If the dog gets frustrated after restarts, lower your total distance goal and build momentum again.

Progressions

Once the Half Dome is reliable, you can increase difficulty by adding environmental distractions, increasing total steps, switching between sit, down, and stand stays, practicing outdoors, or adding handler motions like picking items up or bending over.

Comprehensive Dog Training Glossary

Canine Learning Theory

- **Operant Conditioning** – Learning that occurs based on consequences (reward or punishment).
- **Classical Conditioning** – Associating a neutral stimulus with a meaningful one (e.g., Pavlov's dog).
- **Positive Reinforcement** – Adding something desirable to increase a behavior (e.g., giving a treat).
- **Negative Reinforcement** – Removing something aversive to increase a behavior (e.g., releasing leash pressure).
- **Positive Punishment** – Adding something aversive to decrease a behavior (e.g., leash pop).
- **Negative Punishment** – Removing something desirable to decrease a behavior (e.g., removing attention).
- **Reinforcer** – Any stimulus that increases the likelihood of a behavior repeating.
- **Punisher** – Any stimulus that decreases the likelihood of a behavior repeating.
- **Primary Reinforcer** – A naturally reinforcing stimulus (e.g., food, affection).
- **Secondary Reinforcer** – A learned reinforcer (e.g., clicker sound).
- **Extinction** – The disappearance of a learned behavior when it is no longer reinforced.
- **Extinction Burst** – A temporary increase in behavior when reinforcement is first removed.
- **Shaping** – Reinforcing successive approximations of a desired behavior.
- **Capturing** – Reinforcing a behavior the dog offers naturally without prompting.
- **Luring** – Using a treat or object to guide the dog into a behavior.

- **Prompting** – Providing additional cues or assistance to elicit a behavior.
- **Fading** – Gradually reducing a prompt or cue to build independence.
- **Discrimination** – Learning to distinguish between different cues or environments.
- **Generalization** – Performing a learned behavior in new situations or environments.
- **Habituation** – Decreased response to a repeated, non-threatening stimulus.
- **Sensitization** – Increased response to a repeated stimulus, often due to stress.
- **Desensitization** – Gradual exposure to reduce sensitivity to a stimulus.
- **Counterconditioning** – Changing a dog's emotional response to a stimulus.
- **Flooding** – Overwhelming exposure to a feared stimulus without escape (generally discouraged).
- **Latency** – Time between giving a cue and the dog performing the behavior.
- **Antecedent** – What happens before a behavior (the trigger or cue).
- **Consequence** – What happens after a behavior (reward or punishment).
- **Motivating Operation** – A condition that affects the value of a reinforcer (e.g., hunger increases treat value).
- **Stimulus Control** – When a behavior reliably occurs in response to a specific cue.

Behavior & Communication

- **Threshold** – The point at which a dog begins to react to a stimulus.
- **Trigger** – A stimulus that causes an emotional or behavioral reaction.

Glossary

- **Trigger Stacking** – Accumulated stress from multiple triggers leading to reactivity.
- **Arousal** – The dog's level of excitement or alertness.
- **Over-arousal** – Excessive excitement that impairs learning or control.
- **Reactivity** – Overreactive behavior to stimuli, such as barking or lunging.
- **Aggression** – Threatening or harmful behavior used to gain distance or control.
- **Stress Signals** – Subtle behaviors indicating discomfort (e.g., lip licking, yawning).
- **Displacement Behaviors** – Actions like sniffing, scratching, or yawning that indicate inner conflict.
- **Calming Signals** – Behaviors used by dogs to diffuse tension (e.g., turning head, soft blinking).
- **Engagement** – A dog's voluntary focus and interest in the handler.
- **Learned Helplessness** – A state where the dog stops trying due to perceived lack of control.
- **Bite Inhibition** – A dog's ability to control the strength of its bite.

Obedience & Training Terms

- **Cue** – A signal (verbal, visual, or physical) that asks for a behavior.
- **Command** – Often used interchangeably with cue, though "cue" is preferred in modern training.
- **Marker** – A word or sound (like a clicker) that marks the moment a behavior occurs.
- **Release Cue** – A word (e.g., "Free!") that tells the dog it's okay to move or stop a behavior.
- **Session** – A dedicated period of training activity.
- **Repetition** – Practicing the same behavior multiple times to reinforce learning.
- **Duration** – How long the dog holds a behavior (e.g., stay).

- **Distance** – The space between the dog and the handler while performing a behavior.
- **Distraction** – Environmental challenges during a behavior.
- **Proofing** – Practicing a cue under increasing levels of distraction or difficulty.
- **Errorless Learning** – Structuring training so that mistakes are minimized or avoided.
- **Back-chaining** – Teaching the last part of a sequence first.
- **Forward-chaining** – Teaching a behavior sequence from the beginning.

Training Tools

- **Clicker** – A small device that makes a clicking sound used as a marker.
- **Target Stick** – A stick or pointer used to guide a dog's movement.
- **Mat/Place** – A designated spot the dog is trained to go to and stay on.
- **Long Line** – A long leash (10–30 feet) used for recall or distance work.
- **Treat Pouch** – A bag worn by the handler for quick access to rewards.
- **Head Halter** – A gentle guiding tool that fits around the dog's muzzle.
- **No-Pull Harness** – A harness designed to reduce pulling behavior.
- **Muzzle** – A safety tool that prevents a dog from biting.
- **E-collar / Shock Collar** – An electronic collar delivering stimulations; controversial and often debated.
- **Prong Collar** – A corrective collar with metal prongs; also debated.
- **Flat Collar** – A standard buckle collar.
- **Slip Lead** – A leash and collar combo that tightens with tension.

📋 Husbandry Terms

- **Handling** – The act of physically interacting with a dog for grooming or care.
- **Cooperative Care** – Training the dog to willingly participate in their own care (e.g., nail trims).
- **Desensitization to Grooming** – Gradual exposure to brushing, clippers, or baths.
- **Muzzle Conditioning** – Teaching a dog to willingly wear a muzzle.
- **Crate Training** – Teaching a dog to view a crate as a safe and comfortable space.
- **Tethering** – Securing a dog in one spot using a leash or tie-down (used with supervision).
- **Body Handling** – Getting a dog comfortable being touched (ears, paws, tail, etc.).
- **Vet Desensitization** – Training for positive associations with vet visits.
- **Mat Work** – Teaching the dog to settle or relax on a mat.
- **Touch Consent Cues** – Training a dog to "opt-in" to being handled.

🗣️ Common Obedience Commands

- Sit
- Down
- Stay
- Come / Here
- Wait
- Leave It
- Drop It
- Look / Watch Me
- Touch (nose to hand)
- Place / Mat
- Heel
- Settle
- Free / Release

Index

Introduction

Part 1 – Trust Is the Foundation Built on Consistency

Key Components of Daily Structure (The 5 Pillars)

Index

Tales of Onyx & Omni

Part 3 – Time to Proof (Train, Test, Repeat)

Index

About the Author

Aaron "Yung" Lee is a professional dog trainer, behavior educator, and the creator of Pawfect Practice Training. Known for his no-nonsense teaching style, clear communication, and ability to break down complex behavior into simple steps, Aaron has taught hundreds of handlers how to understand their dogs more deeply and train with purpose.

His work blends science-backed learning theory with practical, real-world application drawn from years of hands-on experience. As a trainer, Aaron specializes in foundational obedience, behavior troubleshooting, and helping everyday dog owners build better structure, routines, and communication with their dogs. His approach focuses on clarity, confidence, and relationship-based training rooted in modern positive reinforcement methods.

Aaron created Pawfect Practice to give dog owners accessible, effective tools that make training easier to understand and implement. From online courses to group classes to this book, his mission is the same: help people build calm, reliable dogs through simple, intentional practice.

When he's not training, writing, or filming educational content, Aaron is studying Animal Biology with the long-term goal of becoming a veterinarian and behavior professional. He lives in California with his two dogs, Canelo and Kona Mae, who continue to shape his work every day.

References

Donaldson, Jean. *The Culture Clash: A Revolutionary New Way to Understand the Relationship Between Humans and Domestic Dogs.* James & Kenneth Publishers, 1997.

Dunbar, Ian. *Before and After Getting Your Puppy: The Positive Approach to Raising a Happy, Healthy, and Well-Behaved Dog.* New World Library, 2007.

McConnell, Patricia. *The Other End of the Leash: Why We Do What We Do Around Dogs.* Ballantine Books, 2002.

Monks of New Skete. *How to Be Your Dog's Best Friend: A Guide to Dog Training.* 3rd ed., Hachette Books, 2001.

Monks of New Skete. *The Art of Raising a Puppy.* Hachette Books, 1997.

Pryor, Karen. *Don't Shoot the Dog: The New Art of Teaching and Training.* Revised ed., Ringpress Books, 2002.

Yin, Sophia. *Perfect Puppy in 7 Days: How to Start Your Puppy off Right.* CattleDog Publishing, 2009.

Dennison, Pamela. *The Complete Idiot's Guide to Positive Dog Training.* Alpha Books, 2006.

www.ingramcontent.com/pod-product-compliance
Lightning Source LLC
Chambersburg PA
CBHW021147130626
46554CB00005B/1696